Tools and Techniques for Effective Data-Driven Decision Making

Philip A. Streifer

With a contribution on leadership by George Goens

ScarecrowEducation
Lanham, Maryland • Toronto • Oxford
2004

Published in the United States of America
by ScarecrowEducation
An imprint of The Rowman & Littlefield Publishing Group, Inc.
4501 Forbes Boulevard, Suite 200, Lanham, Maryland 20706
www.scarecroweducation.com

PO Box 317
Oxford
OX2 9RU, UK

British Library Cataloguing in Publication Information Available

Library of Congress Cataloging-in-Publication Data

Streifer, Philip Alan.
Tools and techniques for effective data-driven decision making / Philip A. Streifer ; with a contribution on leadership by George Goens.
p. cm.
Includes bibliographical references and index.
ISBN 1-57886-123-3 (pbk. : alk. paper)
1. Educational indicators—United States. 2. Educational evaluation—United States. 3. School management and organization—United States. I. Goens, George A. II. Title.

LB2846.S87 2004
371.2'00973—dc22 2004000072

♾™ The paper used in this publication meets the minimum requirements of American National Standard for Information Sciences—Permanence of Paper for Printed Library Materials, ANSI/NISO Z39.48-1992.
Manufactured in the United States of America.

Contents

Chapter One

The New Literacies Required for Data-Driven Decision Making

America's schools could be on the verge of making significant breakthroughs in understanding achievement and designing interventions to improve student growth. Complex organizations have long realized that it is virtually impossible to chart a course of improvement if current levels of performance are not well known and understood. However, our public schools are just now at the dawn of this level of knowledge about achievement. This is not to say that educators have been unaware about the need for accessing reliable data to drive school improvement efforts as they have engaged in school improvement processes for decades. What is different is the emergence of data-driven decision-making tools and techniques to guide and inform these processes.

New approaches to gathering and analyzing data that reduce the query and analysis time from weeks and months to minutes or hours are becoming available to schools. Yet, for all of this technology, we are beginning to run into challenges. For example, some of the new tools do not provide access to all the necessary data to run a query through to its logical conclusion. Other tools are very difficult to use. Still others provide informative reports that seem to beg more questions than they address. In addition, even if one has the right tool, conducting these analyses and properly interpreting the results can be challenging. What is going on?

ASKING THE RIGHT QUESTIONS

The American Association of School Administrators (AASA) has stated that "data driven decision-making is attractive to school leaders, but they do not know how to ask the right questions."[1] At one level, I agree; in fact, my previous book co-published with AASA took that very position, but my further research into this issue reveals that most administrators ask great questions—complex and powerful ones about teaching and learning. Thus, it would appear that the problem is not that school leaders fail to ask the right questions, but that they do not know how to deconstruct their questions into doable analyses (or subqueries) using sound research principles and techniques. This is an important distinction, one that if not solved through training and the development of new decision-support systems, could render this latest round of school improvement efforts another failure in the long list of attempts since *A Nation at Risk*. An even greater problem is that educators do not have access to essential tools to address their most important and complex questions that typically focus on causality—identifying those variables that predict some outcome. Thus, it appears that collectively we are now at the "data admiration stage," ready to move to the next phase—but what will it really take to move from admiration to action?

My work with school leaders on data-driven decision making reveals that too few educators possess the knowledge and skills needed to address these tougher, more complex questions. For example, to address a straightforward question such as "does our early intervention program have a positive impact on elementary school success?" requires a complex set of procedures to answer. It assumes an awful lot about what educators know and can do in this arena of data-driven decision making. My experience tells me that precious few of us know how to answer this question, have access to the resources to have it analyzed, or even have the required data to do the analysis. Many of the so-called data-driven decision-making processes and toolkits used in the field today are excellent overviews of what is required, but most fail on one major point—the assumptions they make about our collective knowledge, skills, and resources to get the job done.

With the passage of No Child Left Behind (NCLB), the problems these deficiencies unveil are quickly coming to the forefront of our attention. For example, all of a sudden a new language is thrust on us: "adequate yearly progress by subgroups." And, as is evident in state after state, these are not simple issues to understand and effectively deal with. They are made complex by the science of psychometrics, the limits of testing, and the politics of accountability.

For example, to know if a school has made adequate yearly progress, we need to begin by disaggregating the data properly. Actually, this is the easiest of the required steps. We then need to ask: How do we actually measure progress from year to year? What is the unit of analysis? Under NCLB, states have two choices in how to do this: they can compare, for example, a school's fourth grade scores from one year to the next, or they can compare the fourth grade cohort to this same group's scores the next year when they become fifth graders, and so on. The latter makes the most sense as it places students at the center of analysis, but it is much more difficult and expensive to implement. Yet even this is not perfect because cohorts will change from year to year due to mobility—in some schools dramatically. The former strategy is by far the easiest method to execute. However, states have the choice to determine how much progress is needed each year with some states taking a "balloon mortgage" type approach, putting off the serious gains that will be necessary until the last four or five years of the law, possibly hoping that NCLB is seriously modified or rescinded by that time.

Even if we could control for student mobility, what about the tests themselves?—how can we confidently compare results over several different measures? If we want to compare math achievement from 2002 fourth grade to 2003 fifth grade, for example, these are often different tests, analyzing different content using different measures. So how do you draw a proper conclusion? Popham[2] reminds us that test validity is mainly a function of what inferences we try to draw from the results. Thus, the question becomes whether the requirements of NCLB—adequate yearly progress—is a proper inference from the data being used? Unless the tests are perfectly aligned—probably not. To avoid these complexities, states will use the same grade to grade comparison (for example, grade four in 2003 vs. grade four in 2004 and so on) for computing adequate yearly progress under NCLB. While this process succeeds at avoiding most of the technical complexities, it results in an interesting policy outcome: the unit of analysis shifts from students to the school.

From the federal policy point of view, this is fine, but what about the schools charged with making improvements? Will the information generated from these analyses help these schools make improvements? In at least one early example, Rhode Island, there was evidence to the contrary, that this policy conflict resulted in schools being left with little, if any, useful data to drive improvements. For example, Providence found itself with virtually no guidance on what to improve when many of its schools were identified as being in need of improvement one year after making significant advancements in student achievement in most of their schools. This setback was due to implementation of tougher standards along with a new form of a very challenging test, the New Standards Reference Exam. This problem was exacerbated because the test yields little diagnostic information for schools to use. Rhode Island modified its early plan to resolve some of the more onerous problems this created.

WHAT ARE THE NEW LITERACIES NEEDED FOR ACHIEVING DATA-DRIVEN DECISION MAKING (DDDM)?

Consider for a moment the knowledge and skills needed by school administrators to properly respond to the federal initiative No Child Left Behind. They need to:

- understand and be able to identify useful performance targets. At the very least, they need to understand how their school's "adequate yearly target" was developed.
- understand and be able to identify useful curriculum benchmarks (or standards) that are aligned to the targets and to their curriculum.
- understand tests and measurements, how to interpret test findings (differentiate among the many score types), and know the limitations and power of these tests.
- be able to deconstruct complex questions into their component parts for analysis.
- possess or acquire the resources to hire the computer and analytic skills to do the longitudinal and disaggregation analyses needed.
- understand systems alignment—how all of these issues interrelate.
- know how to run various analyses and whether they have the correct data required.
- be able to draw reasoned and proper inferences about performance and achievement from the results of these analyses.
- know if these data are readily accessible for analysis and if not, what needs to be done to make them accessible.

This is why data-driven decision making is such a challenge for school leaders and teachers today—it requires a new language and set of skills for the twenty-first "accountability century." Unfortunately, the policy makers are making gross assumptions about our collective knowledge and skills.

If this premise is correct, then we need to back up and start somewhere. One place to start is in understanding the fundamental difference between reporting basic performance results (such as what we will be doing with NCLB) and conducting more complex analyses to help guide intervention strategies.

MAKING DECISIONS

To understand this fundamental issue in data-driven decision making, consider what it is that moves one to take action on an issue. What drives administrative decision-making behavior? A colleague recently noted that Madison Avenue has a knack for packaging a complex idea in a sixty second television commercial—and these ads often persuade us to take action. Is that because our emotions are being manipulated? Maybe. But could it also be that a persuasive argument is being made and that useful information is being presented?

For example, a year ago all of the U.S. automakers offered zero percent financing that sent tens of thousands of us to the showrooms—many of whom made a decision to buy. The automakers' pitch was not very different from before, yet many more of us took this bite of the apple. Why? What can we learn from this example for educational decision making?

In his book, *Making the Grade: Reinventing America's Schools*, Tony Wagner[3] argues that we react to persuasive data, data that point out dramatic differences in achievement between groups or against some standard (like graduation rates). I, too, have found that same phenomenon in my work and would take it a step farther, that sometimes the most persuasive data are not readily observed but are hidden in the sea of information we deal with every day. In astronomy we need more sophisticated procedures and powerful instruments to unveil the true beauties and mysteries of the night sky. The Orion Nebula is not visible to the naked eye, but it is revealed as we look through binoculars, and we see even more detail through an eight-inch telescope, and so on. It is in this detailed view that we learn what this phenomenon really is, a vast area of dust and matter "lit up" by four hot young stars. My work in data-driven decision making reveals the same phenomenon—that when we drill down into the detailed data using more sophisticated analyses, we often uncover new and important information that can be persuasive enough to move us to action. Moreover, when we are presented with persuasive data that addresses a need or concern, we will act. If we need a car, the offer of zero percent financing is enough to move us to a purchase decision rather than having the old buggy fixed.

There is a growing national movement to hold schools and school districts accountable today. The ESEA No Child Left Behind Act of 2001 is adding to that pressure at both the state and local levels. The law (or rather, the state implementation of the federal definition of "adequate yearly progress") will reveal the compelling news—it will identify schools that do not make adequate yearly progress over three-year intervals and, as a result, will be sanctioned in some way. This law will certainly be persuasive, but will it tell us what needs to change even if we are compelled to do so? Returning to our automobile example, many of us passed up on this opportunity, even though we were presented persuasive information about total cost of ownership. Why? It is likely that many of us performed a cost-benefit analysis (Do I really need a new car? How long will mine last? What will it cost even at zero percent interest?) and decided that even such a great deal as this was not worth incurring an unnecessary expense.

For the automobile example, we are capable of performing the cost-benefit analysis because all of the needed information is available. Moreover, we are familiar with these cost-benefit analyses when making major purchase decisions by calculating the pros and cons.

However, what useful detailed data do we have available to calculate "adequate yearly progress" that can lead to meaningful corrective actions? The most useful data we have is a simple "roll-up" or summary report based on aggregate school averages by how one school did versus another. These data tell us little about which students did well over time, which did not, who is contributing to flat performance (impact of mobility), what programs they participated in, and so on.

Since the unit of analysis is now the school, from a simplistic point of view, a straightforward report of how the school did from year to year will suffice—at least from the federal perspective. But to know specifically what to change, we need the detailed or student level data to do more complex, "drill-down" analyses. In my car example, just seeing the commercial will not move me to buy; only after careful analysis of the details, and a comparison of the various options, am I able to make a reasoned decision.

Persuasive data—data that moves us to take corrective action—come in two forms. Primarily, we need to see the big picture, but we also need to know the details about what should be changed—if anything. At that point, we are likely to define and decide what action(s) to take. And, by the way, sometimes a reasonable decision is a conscious one to do nothing.

Thus, at one level, we can see that learning about an issue from a simple summary report or seeing it at a basic level (learning about zero percent financing or seeing the Orion Nebula through binoculars) is the first level of decision making or learning about an issue. However, actions based on deeper learning require more complex analysis found in detailed/student-level data and often require more sophisticated tools and techniques to complete. Just learning that a school is deficient under NCLB analysis will not lead to improvement—specific corrective actions are needed. Deeper analyses of the detailed/student-level data are required to identify just what these corrective actions should be.

A MODEL FOR DDDM

To guide this work I present a three-stage model of data-driven decision making that helps flesh out the reporting to analysis continuum (discussed in full in chapter 3).

Stage I uses aggregate, roll-up data (typically averages or percentages) for reporting school effectiveness, such as in the use of statewide, online school report cards or summary reports from state mastery tests. This is analogous to the TV commercial—it provides a convenient way to see the big picture, how this school is doing compared to others, but it does not provide the detailed information for change if performance is out of the norm.

Stage II uses more in-depth analyses based on detailed, individual student data and includes reporting from these analyses. Many initial conclusions drawn from Stage I reports are often misleading and sometimes wrong when subsequently analyzed more deeply at Stage II (Streifer[4]).

Stage II provides a deeper and clearer picture of performance on specific cohorts and their members; tests performance trends for statistical and practical importance; reduces subgroups to small groups of students—sometimes two and three students or even specific students—who require intervention; isolates cohort members contributing to improvements; and allows for initial program evaluation where logical links between student course grades and standardized test scores exist. At this level of data-driven decision making, more revealing and persuasive findings come to light, such as revealing the birth of stars in the Orion Nebula.

However, for Stage II reports to be truly useful, I have found that all of this number crunching needs to be followed up with observations and interviews to inform our understanding of trends and to identify potential actions. In other words, the analyses provide a useful "compass heading" for one's decisions, but they often do not reveal specific and discernible actions. This may sound curious, if not frustrating, as one would think that after doing all this work the direction and solution should become obvious. Occasionally this does occur, but not often. It's a lot like buying a car: at the end of all the analysis, you are left with a tough personal decision (unless, of course, your auto just hit 200,000 miles and died on the road!).

I have previously written about the role of "informed intuition" in decision making. We are now finding that the summary reporting of performance and achievement results from Stage I analyses do little to inform one's decision-making capability, other than to move one to decide to examine a potential problem more deeply. That, in and of itself, can be very important—a necessary but insufficient condition for effective decision making about what interventions are needed. We are learning that the results of analyses performed at Stage II provided to teachers, followed up with discussion about their relevance, is what is most persuasive and will more likely lead to meaningful actions and change. Chapter 5 will present general case studies to demonstrate this point.

Finally, Stage III is the application of data-mining tools to learn about causality—a topic discussed at length in this book. The reason for such close attention to this issue is that most of the questions I hear from school leaders and teachers are ones of causality. Yet this is a new and emerging field—one that we are just now beginning to explore. Chapter 4 demonstrates what it takes to perform this level of analysis and what we can know about causality given that we are very early in the development of these tools and techniques.

Thus, the purpose of this book is to explain, by example, what can be learned about student achievement at Stages I, II, and III with a focus on what is knowable at the causality stage and what it takes to get this work done.

SUMMARY

We make many decisions in our daily lives, some quick and easy, some tough and drawn out. We are learning that arriving at decisions about improving achievement is challenging work because the variables are not that clear, often missing or unmatched with those we want to compare, and the analyses needed to gain actionable information are hard and complicated. Fortunately, there are tools available to help, but this work requires a new set of literacies. Interestingly, even when this work is conducted properly, one is often left with a better sense of "informed intuition" about what to do, but not with an absolute, certain direction.

What we can say at this point is that the review of summary Stage I reports is not likely to significantly inform our intuition or guide decision making. However, it is a necessary first step to decide what to investigate more deeply. Interestingly, No Child Left Behind reports are at the Stage I level. To use another analogy, it's like going to the general physician who performs a basic examination and then decides to send you to a specialist to investigate a particular symptom. Without this necessary first step, we don't know what specialist to go to, which can result in a waste of precious time and resources. Similarly, NCLB analyses need to learn specifically what improvements are critical. To achieve the promise of NCLB, we must proceed to Stage II at least. It is in Stage II that we may find data that can truly guide decision making if performed properly and interpreted correctly.

Thus, Stage I reports may uncover persuasive trends that prompt us to reinvestigate the data for hidden truths that will guide intervention strategies—Stage II. Many of the questions educators seek answers to are questions of causality. Neither Stage I nor Stage II analyses can reach causality—Stage III techniques and tools are needed. Even then, research is demonstrating that we rarely obtain a definitive answer to our question. The best we seem to do is to limit the range of possibilities.

I used to believe that if we could put all of a district's data into one large relational database, we could learn precisely what to change to promote improvement. Having worked with many of these databases, I have learned that this is just not the case. Number crunching will not lead to precise actionable steps—but it will set a direction for further discussion with teachers about what should be done. In addition, within this framework exists the true value of data-driven decision making—as a tool to help determine a starting point for these discussions.

Thus, my goal in writing this book is to provide guidance on these issues—to explain what is knowable about improving schools and achievement within a data-rich environment. I will explicate the new literacies required for this work in order to help others avoid the pitfalls of making poor decisions.

NOTES

1. American Association of School Administrators. *Data Driven Decision Making: What's Working* [Brochure] (Alexandria, Va.: 2002).
2. W. J. Popham, *The Truth About Testing* (Alexandria, Va.: Association for Supervision and Curriculum Development, 2001).
3. T. Wagner and T. Vander Ark, *Making the Grade: Reinventing America's Schools* (New York: Routledge Falmer, 2001).
4. P. A. Streifer, *Using Data to Make Better Educational Decisions* (Lanham, Md.: Scarecrow Education with the American Association of School Administrators, 2002).

Chapter Two

Data-Driven Decision Making—Where Are We Today? State of the Technology

STATE OF THE ART

It is not easy to run simple data-driven decision-making queries. The technology is unrefined and data are typically too messy. Consider for a moment the impact of student mobility on reported achievement scores for your school. How can you tell the extent to which student mobility (in and out over the year) affects the scores that are reported in the newspapers? What about that impact on NCLB—how is adequate yearly progress computed and which students impact your results the most? No doubt in some schools the impact is negligible, that is, most kids are in the school all year long, but in some schools the impact can be dramatic when there are high incidences of mobility. In any event, unless you run the query, you will never know. So, what's involved in actually "knowing"?

WHAT IT TAKES TO RUN AN APPARENTLY SIMPLE QUERY

Given the "state of the art" of modern computer technology, it is difficult (and expensive!) to program, for example, a single "mobility" button into a decision-support/data warehousing system that, when pressed, yields the answer. Even if you have one of these systems for your school, this query (and many others) often require several steps to complete (such as the examples that will be explored later in this book). Because many steps are required to complete these analyses, as important as they are, they are not often run. The problem is a function of today's technology coupled with what school districts can afford, along with the typical issues associated with messy school data.

THE PROBLEM OF MESSY DATA

School data can be (and often are!) messy and incomplete. For example, to run a mobility query for sixth grade, we need to know the accurate list of students in the school at either the beginning of sixth grade (preferably at the end of fifth) and the accurate list at the time of the test administration (let's say in May). Since the purpose is to determine how students performed who spent the entire year in school disaggregated from those in attendance for only part of the year, we need to create two groups: "Present All Year" and "Present Part of the Year."

The problem I find with most school data is that schools typically drop from their student information systems students who leave during the year, sometimes re-assigning that student's ID to another student. When this happens, all electronic records of the first student are lost. Frankly, I am surprised to see how often this happens.

Even if you have all of these records saved, you will need to sort the data by date in the student registration (database) table. Thus, we will want to retrieve, on one list, all students enrolled from the first to the last day of school and, on the second list, any student who was enrolled for some lesser amount of time and the dates of that attendance. That can require a sophisticated set of commands for the query engine (of the database) depending on what system you are using. To complicate matters even further, at this point it is possible to find that the database field containing this attendance information for each child is not properly formatted as a date/time field—the wrong format would make the sort impossible.

To resolve some of these problems, several vendors of data warehousing systems create special database tables that resolve these issues for running a mobility query. But doing so requires a fair amount of data cleanup and can become expensive. Unless you do the cleanup or have it done for you, running the mobility query is going to be a nightmare.

DATA INTEGRITY

The problem of data availability and integrity is crucial to running several important queries. For many smaller school districts without management information system (MIS) departments, these problems are common. I have even seen larger districts experience these problems as their MIS staff are typically overworked and do not have the time to clean up all of these data. Moreover, these problems are made even more complex if the school has changed the student information system it uses over the years (as combining data from one system to another can become very complex). An equally important problem exists if you want to run a mobility query across several years—this requires drawing data from two schools' databases where each may use different student systems or even the same system but the data have not been integrated.

Unfortunately, these are real problems facing school leaders as they attempt to run important queries, such as determining the impact of student mobility on achievement. The state of the art today is problematic: the systems to run the query cannot be easily programmed to achieve a direct response, nor are the data typically in tip-top shape. Thus, running these queries requires time, patience, and skill.

THE PROMISE OF THE SCHOOL INTEROPERABILITY FRAMEWORK (SIF)

There is help on the horizon. Many school MIS directors are realizing that they need to capture and retain student IDs and teacher IDs, and create uniform course IDs across schools. Most data warehousing systems, which are becoming more affordable, are including specially designed data tables (created by changing or transforming your raw data) to assist in these more complicated queries, such as mobility. And finally, there is the School Interoperability Framework (SIF)[1] initiative that is working to standardize school data across disparate systems and enable more reliable data transfers from system to system.

For the short term, though, your more complicated queries will require patience and skill due to the inherent messiness of school data and the limits of the technology. Over time these problems will be resolved, but not for the immediate future.

USING AVAILABLE TOOLS TO DO THIS WORK

Working with an affluent school district recently, where the staff are very data driven in their approach to school improvement, I was impressed with the analyses that they had been conducting. Their testing and evaluation director had been disaggregating several of the state mastery test data for the district's schools with many of the schools themselves running further analyses. When I asked what tools they were using, almost all of them said "paper and pencil," "calculators," and a few said "Microsoft Excel." Regarding the latter, I asked how they had entered the data into Excel. Puzzled at the question, they said that they had entered it all by hand!

This characterizes the state of the art for most of the districts with whom I have worked or spoken over the past few years. No doubt, this labor-intensive approach seriously handicaps the extent to which educators can explore relationships between inputs (such as program enhancements, resources, instructional techniques, and materials) and outcomes. I will have more to say on the problems this situation creates in responding to accountability demands in chapter 6, but suffice it to say for now that working under these conditions is analogous to trying to diagnose a serious medical condition with mid-twentieth-century medicine.

ORGANIZING ACCESS TO ALL OF YOUR DATA

The most significant challenge schools face today in doing data-driven decision making is organizing their data in ways and into systems that make them accessible and query-able. Time is a critical factor—if you have to take hours and days to collect and organize the data, you are probably not going to run the query. Even if you do, you will be frustrated down the road, as is often the case when one query leads to several others requiring access to even more data (for example, after examining the mobility impact, we may want to know if achievement was further impacted by attendance or if poor performance could have been detected earlier by previous test scores or school performance). Thus, it is important to have immediate access to as much of these detailed student data as possible to run a query through to its logical conclusion or to the point where the data for follow-up queries do not exist.

DATA WAREHOUSES AND HOW THEIR DESIGNS IMPACT YOUR QUERIES

The solution to many of these challenges is the data warehouse. Data warehouses come in several configurations, some better for certain types of queries than others. Basically there are three configurations: (1) the full "open-architecture" data warehouse; (2) the constrained, "closed-architecture" data warehouse; and (3) the "data cube" (a derivative of the data warehouse) which provides access to a more limited set of data in a preformatted configuration. Each of these systems has advantages and disadvantages. The difficulty and challenge of implementing a properly designed system for your needs should not be underestimated,[2] but a well-fitted system can work wonders for your school improvement efforts.

DATA WAREHOUSING SYSTEM TYPES—PROS AND CONS: SELECTING THE RIGHT SYSTEM

Open Architecture

The most useful data warehouse is the full open-architecture system because all of your data, regardless of source and type, can be loaded for use in querying and new data can be easily added at any time with minimal or no extra cost. These systems have come down in cost, whereas five or more years ago even a basic system could cost upwards of $250,000 for a relatively small school district (around 10,000 students). That same system is now available for far less, with prices ranging from $4 to $10 per student depending on how much functionality you initially purchased.

These cost savings have been realized with more powerful, yet less expensive, databases, query engines, and web technologies. The advantage to this type of system is that it can hold all of your data, making dynamic querying only a function of user knowledge and skill.

This unlimited query access is often referred to as the ability to run ad hoc queries. These systems can provide 24×7 web access to your entire database for unlimited querying and reporting. The downside is that the query engines used by these systems are harder to learn than in some of the other systems I will describe. Some vendors are providing the full ad hoc query access plus the ability to post completed queries (as in the form of an Executive Level Information System) to secure websites for easy review by staff who do not have the time to learn the ad hoc query process. The trade-off between this type of system and others is power vs. ease of use.

Closed-Architecture and Hybrid Systems

The closed-architecture data warehouse takes selected data from your district and fits or maps it to the vendor's predesigned database structure. The advantage to this system is that the core database structure is fixed, no matter whose data are being loaded. Thus, to the end user, data from district A will look the same as data from district B. The remapping process can force users to employ the vendor's definitions for the data elements. Obviously, the data from both districts are secure from one another, but the underlying structures are identical, unlike some open-architecture systems where the structures will be different and more fully reflect what the district has been familiar with.

At least one vendor has created the best of both worlds—a fixed data model that is so robust that virtually any school data can be mapped into the system. This example can be considered a hybrid—both fixed yet capable of handling all data—thus taking advantage of the benefits of both systems.

What is the difference? Let's say that your school uses a unique system of computing grade point average (GPA). In fact, you may use several forms of GPA—weighted, unweighted, and you may calculate this quarterly. In an open-architecture system, all of this data can easily be loaded. In the fixed system, there may not be a place for the quarterly unweighted GPA—it may be either dropped, not loaded, or it may be mapped to a field called "nonstandard" GPA.

However, the advantage that the closed/fixed-architecture system has is the ability of the vendor to develop predefined queries that can run no matter what district is using the system, which cuts the cost of delivering these reports. In some of these systems, the vendor, not the district personnel, actually runs the query. For example, the district might call the vendor, ask them to run a query on mobility for a particular year and cohort of students, and receive the results in a day or two.

There is at least one major disadvantage to closed-architecture systems. They typically do not as easily (or affordably) accept all of your data as the open-architecture system—you would have to pay extra for that quarterly unweighted GPA to be loaded or to add your own school-based testing data. However, this is not a problem of the hybrid systems—a system that has all the advantages of both closed and open-architecture systems. As the technology advances, more vendors will certainly adopt this design structure.

Data Cube

The third option, and a fairly popular one, is the system built around the data-cube design. The technical name for this version is the OLAP design. OLAP stands for online analytical processing. These specially designed systems take subsets of data and design them into hierarchical relationships. These designs are fixed, like the fixed-architecture system described above, but they too can be reengineered to accommodate more data over time (at additional costs). Once these hierarchical data relationships are designed, the user is given access via a web interface that is fairly easy to use and often allows for graphic data representations. Both of the previous data warehouse designs (open- and closed-architecture) also allow for graphic representations of data, but the data cube is particularly strong in this regard.

The disadvantage to the data-cube design is that it is, for all intents and purposes, a very fixed design, and querying ability is limited to the hierarchical relationships that the designer built into the system. If your ad hoc query requires comparing two data elements that are not logically linked in this hierarchical relationship, you are out of luck.

However, the advantage to these systems are: (1) ease of use—they are particularly easy to use, even for novice users; (2) they are web accessible; and (3) they are particularly strong in disaggregating data along the predefined hierarchical relationships designed into the system.

SELECTING THE RIGHT SYSTEM

Selecting the system that is right for you ultimately depends on what you want to do with it. I advise school districts to make a list of the queries they want to run (a comprehensive list—see chapter 3 for a discussion on how this plays out) and then determine the utility vs. cost of a system by whether it can address the majority of these queries, what it will cost, and how difficult it is to use. You will also need to ask about the process of adding new data, how often you can refresh the existing data, and the associated costs for these updates.

As to ease of use, none of these systems are simple—ease of use here is a relative term. Nevertheless, some systems are, in fact, easier to use than others. To take advantage of the first system—open architecture—you will need a staff that has three skill sets:

(1) someone who knows their way around a computer (I use the example of someone who buys a new program, loads it, and gets it running without ever looking at the Users' Manual);
(2) someone who knows your data (again, by example, someone who knows that the names/codes for algebra courses might not be the same across schools or knows that the "standard" score is different from the "raw" score and how it is different); and
(3) someone who knows and can run basic statistics.

Many districts that have these systems assign full ad hoc query access to a few advanced users who have most or all of these skills and who can then create queries/reports and post them for other staff to view.

Finally, if you want to provide all of your users access to some of the data for basic data disaggregation, the data cube is the way to go. However, not all of your queries can be run with these systems (fixed-architecture and/or data-cube) regardless of who is using it (hybrid systems aside). Again, the final selection of a decision-support system and data warehouse should be based on a cost-benefit analysis of the questions you have and whether the system can adequately address those questions.

INDEPENDENT REVIEWS

Available tools have been reviewed by several agencies and publications. The American Association of School Administrators performed an early review in April 2001.[3] *Scholastic Administrator* has a buying guide in their September 2003 journal.[4] A more comprehensive review can be found both in print and on the web at www.csos.jhu.edu/systemics/datause.htm—a service of the Johns Hopkins University Center for Research on the Education of Students Placed At Risk.[5]

RECOMMENDATION

With all of the decision-support and data-warehousing system options available, what design should you select for your data-driven decision-making needs? To answer this question, consider the fact that all of the examples used in this book are real questions that have been asked by school leaders and were analyzed using either an open-architecture data-warehousing system or were done by hand. In their original form, they could *not* have been answered using either a typical closed-architecture or data-cube system.

I had the opportunity to work on a closed-architecture system several years ago, developed by a corporate leader in the data-warehousing business. The system worked under certain conditions, but it had two major flaws that prevented it from being truly useful. First, due to the manner in which the system was built (an analogy is the "behind-the-scenes plumbing" or programming used), it would return a "No Data to Fetch" error in response to certain queries. This happened when the fixed "plumbing" passed through a data table that had not been populated with a particular district's data (a data table is where the actual data reside in a computer database and databases contain many data tables all linked through some logical structure). It's somewhat like your home water plumbing system trying to run through a pipe with a big hole in it—the water leaks and nothing comes out of the faucet.

Figure 2.1 shows how a database is designed (a basic example, but useful in this context). In this design, we have several data tables containing various data elements or fields. Using this simple database, we could

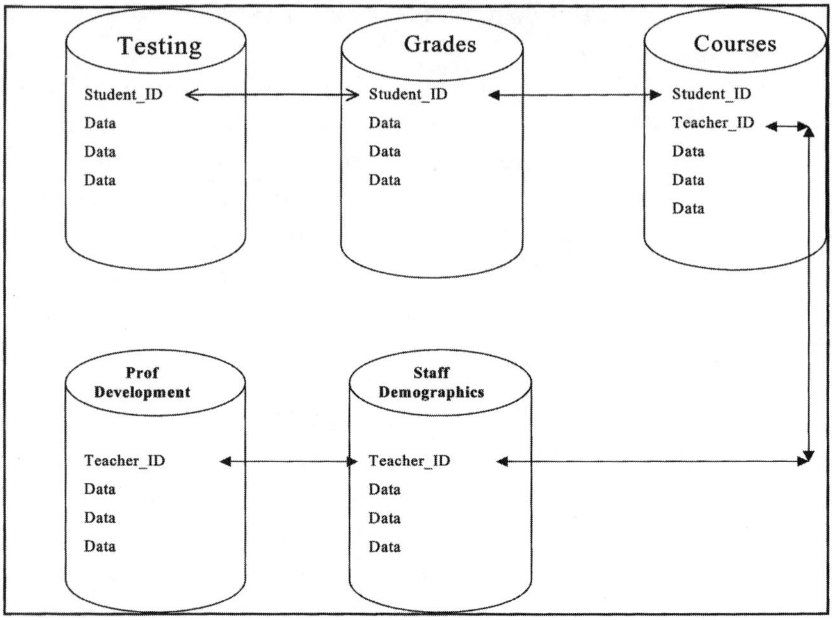

Figure 2.1. Typical Data Model Linking Structure

explore a range of relationships between student test scores, class grades, teacher background, and staff development activities attended. But if the staff demographics data table was empty, or not populated, the computer would have no way to link to teacher professional development because the linking field, "teacher ID," would not be populated in that table.

In a fixed architectural system, this table would exist in the database regardless of whether you put data into it. And if you did not "populate" it (give those data to the vendor), your query would crash if it attempted to go through that table.

In an open-architecture system, the vendor would realize that you did not populate that table and they would custom design the database to eliminate that data table. In this case they would link the course teacher table ID directly to the professional development table teacher ID.

Here is another example of how this problem plays out: When I wanted to get a list of courses that students had taken in the math department along with their math mastery test scores, a "No Data to Fetch" error would result if the district had incomplete information on which courses were linked to the department codes. In other words, the district had populated the database with the students' names, their mastery scores, and what courses each student took, but had not linked every course to a department code. When the computer tried to pull up courses by department code, the system crashed. It is interesting to note that this issue of missing department codes is a common problem with school data—one of those problems associated with data messiness discussed earlier. You should discuss these problems with vendors to determine the extent to which they may be resolved. Vendors are beginning to solve these problems by engineering very specialized plumbing designed around the unique characteristics of school data.

ADDING NEW DATA

Another frustration I found with my early fixed-architecture system cropped up every time a district wanted to add data not already included in the core design. For example, several districts wanted to add their own "off-level" mastery test scores to this system, but the core design had not accounted for all of these different test types. To add these data required major restructuring of the database that, due to cost, were often put off to the next version release—six to twelve months down the road. This was not very satisfying to the district users who had pressing questions requiring the use of these data now.

As a result of these issues, I began working with open-architecture systems that allow for the easy addition of new data at any time and also never result in a "No Data to Fetch" error because each district's system is designed around the data that are loaded, not by trying to fit their data into a predesigned, limited architecture.

I am oversimplifying the technology here to make my point. There are ways around these problems in the design structure of the data warehouse. However, you need to ask the vendor how to resolve these problems and the cost and performance consequences of this approach.

The research and examples presented in this book could not have been run with most closed or fixed systems or with most data-cube models because each of the districts have very different data sets requiring unique databases to meet their needs and to run successful queries. As we will see in the next section on what knowledge is needed to do this work, the best place to determine which system is right for you is to start with the questions your school leaders ask since they know best the important (and contextual) questions to improving student achievement in their school. These questions almost always require access to data elements selected from among all the data domains that are collected by a district. In general, when you try to fit your data into some predetermined design, the system will not work or will have to be re-engineered at increasing cost to accommodate all of those data.

Finally, data cubes limit the users' queries to not only the data that have been loaded, but to the hierarchical relationships built into the system. Cube systems are very useful, however, if you keep in mind what they were designed for. These systems make exploration of selected data elements and their relationship to other selected data elements extremely easy to accomplish. Thus, if you want to give users some control over an easy-to-use system, albeit limited in what queries it can run, then the data cube is a good option. Several vendors are now packaging data cubes with other report options to expand the usefulness of the overall system.

Once a decision-support system is selected, what can be done with them in the larger sense: that is, what are these systems' inherent strengths and limitations in total? As we will see in the next section, no matter what system you have, each one has certain limitations in terms of what it can do as measured against our expectations. Throughout this discussion a basic gap emerges between our desired reporting needs and the analyses needed to create them. Unfortunately, none of these systems are as good as they need to be for many of our analyses.

THE FUTURE OF REPORTING VS. ANALYSIS

To help understand what we can and cannot do today in terms of reporting school data, and to demonstrate the difference between data analysis and reporting, consider the following sequence of charts. The first (figure 2.2) is a rather common chart replicating the weather page found in most newspapers. This chart tells us a great deal of information. You can quickly scan it to find your weather by region as it is easy to read, providing a vast amount of information on one chart, color-coded data variants (in this case by temperature), and, perhaps most interesting of all, providing a forecast—a prediction of what is to come based on very sophisticated regression modeling.

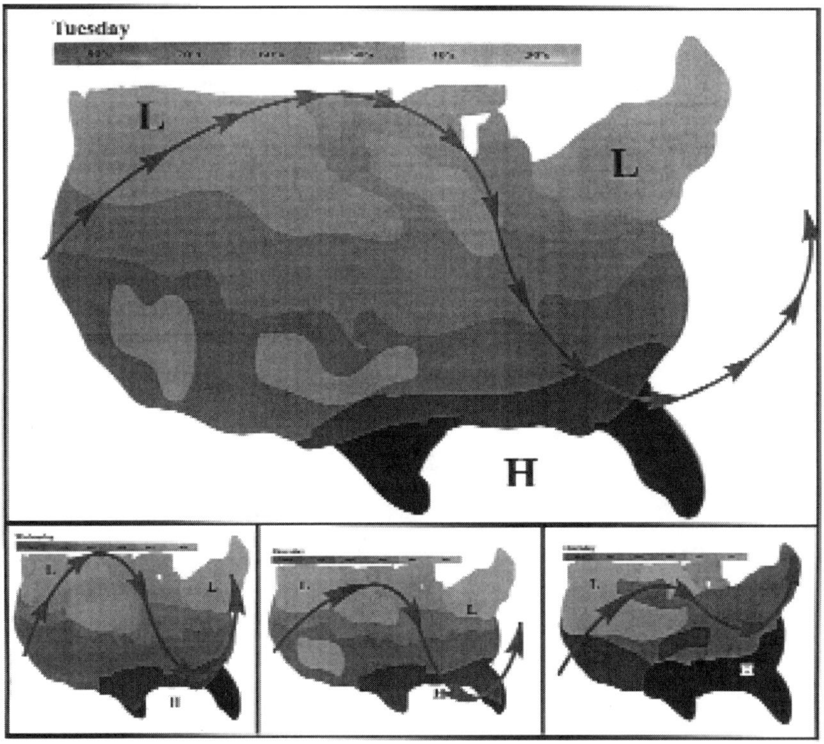

Figure 2.2. U.S. Weather Map

Now, consider a second example—the stock market pages (figure 2.3). This is nothing more than a listing of hundreds of stocks with a select set of information about each stock. It has been collected from several sources and some analytics have been performed to create various data points, for example, to determine the P/E ratio. Basically, however, it is just a list of disparate stocks that is hard to understand unless you really know what you are looking for and have been schooled in the world of Wall Street.

The third example, figure 2.4, represents the middle ground between the first two examples, figures 2.2 and 2.3. This chart shows the summary, or roll-up results of several stock indexes on a given day in November 2002. (By the way, the first segment of this chart—the Dow Jones Industrial Average—is not really an average. It is an index or compilation of thirty notable stocks. Actually, it is the sum value of those stocks. So, for example, if General Motors stock were to rise 2.0 points on a day, and no other stock in the Dow Jones Average changed that day, then the total

STOCK EXCHANGE

YTD % CHG	YEAR HI	YEAR LO	STOCK SYM	DIV	YLD%	PE	VOL 100s	CLOSE	NET CHG
-2.7	14.59	5.02	TelLeste TBE	0	1.1	...	50	13.5	0.05
2	29.99	12.09	TelNrdCelu TND	.46e	...	...	68	28.5	-0.5
-2	11.2	4.45	TelNoCelu TCN	0	1.6	...	46	10.7	-0.04
0.1	23.7	15.54	TJX Cos TJX	0.14	0.6	20	2918	22.08	0.11
0	22.09	10.6	TRC Cos TRR	0	...	29	410	21.06	0.06
2	29.99	12.09	TelNrdCelu TND	.46e	...	...	68	28.5	-0.5
-2	11.2	4.45	TelNoCelu TCN	0	1.6	...	46	10.7	-0.04
6.2	16.49	6.38	TelNoLeste TNE	.80e	...	...	13383	16.38	-0.11
-2.7	14.59	5.02	TelLeste TBE	0	1.1	...	50	13.5	0.05
0.1	23.7	15.54	TJX Cos TJX	0.14	0.6	20	2918	22.08	0.11
0	9.8	3.79	TV Acteca ADS TZA s	.75e	8.2	11	6898	9.1	-0.03
0.9	23.98	15	TXU TXU	0.5	2.1	dd	11914	23.93	0.06
6.6	12.93	5.89	TaiwanSemi TSM	stk	...	...	61438	10.92	0.01
1.2	1.2	1.2	TEKNIP TKP	1.2	1.2	1.2	1.2	1.2	1.2
3.7	27.88	14.3	TEKNIP TKP	.90e	3.2	...	64	27.92	0.08
0.7	24.56	13.43	TECHNITROL TNL	0	...	43	1441	20.89	-0.43
4	21.43	15.6	TAUBMANCtr TCO	1.08f	5	...	5840	21.42	0.16
0.6	52.25	36.5	TCF Fnl TCB	1.3	2.5	17	5921	51.66	0.59
1.7	73.4	32.4	TDK Cp ADS TDK	.45e	0.6	...	183	73.01	-0.39
0	9.8	3.79	TV Acteca ADS TZA s	.75e	8.2	11	6898	9.1	-0.03
0.9	23.98	15	TXU TXU	0.5	2.1	dd	11914	23.93	0.06
3.7	27.88	14.3	TEKNIP TKP	.90e	3.2	...	64	27.92	0.08
0	14.99	15.7	TelCeluSul TSU	.23e	0.5	...	247	14.35	-0.35
6.6	12.93	5.89	TaiwanSemi TSM	stk	...	...	61438	10.92	0.01
0.9	23.98	15	TXU TXU	0.5	2.1	dd	11914	23.93	0.06
-2.7	14.59	5.02	TelLeste TBE	0	1.1	...	50	13.5	0.05
2	29.99	12.09	TelNrdCelu TND	.46e	...	...	68	28.5	-0.5
-2	11.2	4.45	TelNoCelu TCN	0	1.6	...	46	10.7	-0.04
0.7	24.56	13.43	TECHNITROL TNL	0	...	43	1441	20.89	-0.43
1.3	38.65	22	TALBOTS TLB	0.4	1.3	16	2514	31.17	0.37
0.9	23.98	15	TXU TXU	0.5	2.1	dd	11914	23.93	0.06
0.7	24.56	13.43	TECHNITROL TNL	0	...	43	1441	20.89	-0.43
4	21.43	15.6	TAUBMANCtr TCO	1.08f	5	...	5840	21.42	0.16
14.4	21.78	8.31	TelNoCelu TCN	0	1.6	...	26720	22.06	0.34
-2.7	14.59	5.02	TelLeste TBE	0	1.1	...	50	13.5	1.2
2	29.99	12.09	TelNrdCelu TND	.46e	...	...	68	28.5	-2.7
-2	11.2	4.45	TelNoCelu TCN	0	1.6	...	46	10.7	4
0.1	23.7	15.54	TJX Cos TJX	0.14	0.6	20	2918	22.08	0.06
0	22.09	10.6	TRC Cos TRR	0	...	29	410	21.06	0.01
2	29.99	12.09	TelNrdCelu TND	.46e	...	...	68	28.5	0.08
-2	11.2	4.45	TelNoCelu TCN	0	1.6	...	46	10.7	-0.43
6.2	16.49	6.38	TelNoLeste TNE	.80e	...	...	13383	16.38	0.16
-2.7	14.59	5.02	TelLeste TBE	0	1.1	...	50	13.5	0.61
0.1	23.7	15.54	TJX Cos TJX	0.14	0.6	20	2918	22.08	0.59
0	9.8	3.79	TV Acteca ADS TZA s	.75e	8.2	11	6898	9.1	-0.39
0.9	23.98	15	TXU TXU	0.5	2.1	dd	11914	23.93	0.11
6.6	12.93	5.89	TaiwanSemi TSM	stk	...	...	61438	10.92	0.05
1.2	1.2	1.2	TEKNIP TKP	1.2	1.2	1.2	1.2	1.2	-0.5
3.7	27.88	14.3	TEKNIP TKP	.90e	3.2	...	64	27.92	-0.04
0.7	24.56	13.43	TECHNITROL TNL	0	...	43	1441	20.89	-0.11
4	21.43	15.6	TAUBMANCtr TCO	1.08f	5	...	5840	21.42	0.34
0.6	52.25	36.5	TCF Fnl TCB	1.3	2.5	17	5921	51.66	0.11
1.7	73.4	32.4	TDK Cp ADS TDK	.45e	0.6	...	183	73.01	0.06
0	9.8	3.79	TV Acteca ADS TZA s	.75e	8.2	11	6898	9.1	-0.03
0.9	23.98	15	TXU TXU	0.5	2.1	dd	11914	23.93	0.06
3.7	27.88	14.3	TEKNIP TKP	.90e	3.2	...	64	27.92	0.01
0	14.99	15.7	TelCeluSul TSU	.23e	0.5	...	247	14.35	0.37
6.6	12.93	5.89	TaiwanSemi TSM	stk	...	...	61438	10.92	0.06
0.9	23.98	15	TXU TXU	0.5	2.1	dd	11914	23.93	0.01
-2.7	14.59	5.02	TelLeste TBE	0	1.1	...	50	13.5	0.08
2	29.99	12.09	TelNrdCelu TND	.46e	...	...	68	28.5	-0.35
-2	11.2	4.45	TelNoCelu TCN	0	1.6	...	46	10.7	0.02
0.7	24.56	13.43	TECHNITROL TNL	0	...	43	1441	20.89	0.05
1.3	38.65	22	TALBOTS TLB	0.4	1.3	16	2514	31.17	0.11
0.9	23.98	15	TXU TXU	0.5	2.1	dd	11914	23.93	-0.03
0.7	24.56	13.43	TECHNITROL TNL	0	...	43	1441	20.89	0.06
4	21.43	15.6	TAUBMANCtr TCO	1.08f	5	...	5840	21.42	0.01
14.4	21.78	8.31	TelNoCelu TCN	0	1.6	...	26720	22.06	0.06

YTD % CHG	YEAR HI	YEAR LO	STOCK SYM	DIV	YLD%	PE	VOL 100s	CLOSE	NET CHG
0.6	52.25	36.5	TCF Fnl TCB	1.3	2.5	17	5921	51.66	0.59
1.7	73.4	32.4	TDK Cp ADS TDK	.45e	0.6	...	183	73.01	-0.39
0.1	23.7	15.54	TJX Cos TJX	0.14	0.6	20	2918	22.08	0.11
0	22.09	10.6	TRC Cos TRR	0	...	29	410	21.06	0.06
0	9.8	3.79	TV Acteca ADS TZA	.75e	8.2	11	6898	9.1	-0.03
0.9	23.98	15	TXU TXU	0.5	2.1	dd	11914	23.93	0.06
6.6	12.93	5.89	TaiwanSemi TSM	stk	...	...	61438	10.92	0.01
1.3	38.65	22	TALBOTS TLB	0.4	1.3	16	2514	31.17	0.37
2.8	59.66	36.23	TalismnEngy TLN	.80fg	1.4	7	1306	58.18	-1.32
2.4	43	28.8	TANGER SKT	2.46	5.9	34	693	41.69	-0.36
0.4	41.8	32.74	TARGET TGT	0.28	0.7	21	50078	39.57	1.17
1.3	11.3	7.2	TASTYBak TBC	0.2	2	dd	138	10.24	0.09
1.8	27.2	14.2	Tatnef ADS TNT	.06e	0.3	...	172	23.22	-0.27
4	21.43	15.6	TAUBMANCtr TCO	1.08f	5	...	5840	21.42	0.16
8.3	19.1	10.45	TDC ADS TLD	.84e	4.3	...	60	19.66	0.61
0.9	23.98	15	TXU TXU	0.5	2.1	dd	11914	23.93	0.06
6.6	12.93	5.89	TaiwanSemi TSM	stk	...	...	61438	10.92	0.01
3.7	27.88	14.3	TEKNIP TKP	.90e	3.2	...	64	27.92	0.08
0.7	24.56	13.43	TECHNITROL TNL	0	...	43	1441	20.89	-0.43
1.2	17	19.47	TecoEngy TE	0.76	5.2	dd	10742	14.58	0.01
1.2	58.75	35.6	TKSHIPS TK	1.00f	1.7	11	4535	57.7	1.8
1.2	4.85	3.02	TEFRON TFR	0	...	...	32	4.38	-0.05
-2.7	41.95	23.7	TEJONRNCH TRC	0		dd	193	39.9	-0.36
4	32.9	15.65	TEKTRONIX TEK	0.16	...	60	6900	32.85	...
0	14.99	15.7	TelCeluSul TSU	.23e	0.5	...	247	14.35	-0.35
7.4	10.75	3.37	TelCntrOest TRO	.12e	1.6	...	4441	10.58	0.02
-2.7	14.59	5.02	TelLeste TBE	0	1.1	...	50	13.5	0.05
2	29.99	12.09	TelNrdCelu TND	.46e	...	...	68	28.5	-0.5
-2	11.2	4.45	TelNoCelu TCN	0	1.6	...	46	10.7	-0.04
6.2	16.49	6.38	TelNoLeste TNE	.80e	...	...	13383	16.38	-0.11
6	12.8	7.7	TelSudCelu TSD	.21e	4.9	...	287	12.04	0.34
0.1	23.7	15.54	TJX Cos TJX	0.14	0.6	20	2918	22.08	0.11
0	22.09	10.6	TRC Cos TRR	0	...	29	410	21.06	0.06
0	9.8	3.79	TV Acteca ADS TZA	.75e	8.2	11	6898	9.1	-0.03
-2.7	14.59	5.02	TelLeste TBE	0	1.1	...	50	13.5	0.05
2	29.99	12.09	TelNrdCelu TND	.46e	...	...	68	28.5	-0.5
-2	11.2	4.45	TelNoCelu TCN	0	1.6	...	46	10.7	-0.04
0.1	23.7	15.54	TJX Cos TJX	0.14	0.6	20	2918	22.08	0.11
0	22.09	10.6	TRC Cos TRR	0	...	29	410	21.06	0.06
2	29.99	12.09	TelNrdCelu TND	.46e	...	...	68	28.5	-0.5
-2	11.2	4.45	TelNoCelu TCN	0	1.6	...	46	10.7	-0.04
6.2	16.49	6.38	TelNoLeste TNE	.80e	...	...	13383	16.38	-0.11
-2.7	14.59	5.02	TelLeste TBE	0	1.1	...	50	13.5	0.05
0.1	23.7	15.54	TJX Cos TJX	0.14	0.6	20	2918	22.08	0.11
0	9.8	3.79	TV Acteca ADS TZA s	.75e	8.2	11	6898	9.1	-0.03
0.9	23.98	15	TXU TXU	0.5	2.1	dd	11914	23.93	0.06
6.6	12.93	5.89	TaiwanSemi TSM	stk	...	...	61438	10.92	0.01
1.2	1.2	1.2	TEKNIP TKP	1.2	1.2	1.2	1.2	1.2	1.2
3.7	27.88	14.3	TEKNIP TKP	.90e	3.2	...	64	27.92	0.08
0.7	24.56	13.43	TECHNITROL TNL	0	...	43	1441	20.89	-0.43
4	21.43	15.6	TAUBMANCtr TCO	1.08f	5	...	5840	21.42	0.16
0.6	52.25	36.5	TCF Fnl TCB	1.3	2.5	17	5921	51.66	0.59
1.7	73.4	32.4	TDK Cp ADS TDK	.45e	0.6	...	183	73.01	-0.39
0	9.8	3.79	TV Acteca ADS TZA s	.75e	8.2	11	6898	9.1	-0.03
0.9	23.98	15	TXU TXU	0.5	2.1	dd	11914	23.93	0.06
3.7	27.88	14.3	TEKNIP TKP	.90e	3.2	...	64	27.92	0.08
0	14.99	15.7	TelCeluSul TSU	.23e	0.5	...	247	14.35	-0.35
6.6	12.93	5.89	TaiwanSemi TSM	stk	...	...	61438	10.92	0.01
0.9	23.98	15	TXU TXU	0.5	2.1	dd	11914	23.93	0.06
-2.7	14.59	5.02	TelLeste TBE	0	1.1	...	50	13.5	0.05
2	29.99	12.09	TelNrdCelu TND	.46e	...	...	68	28.5	-0.5
-2	11.2	4.45	TelNoCelu TCN	0	1.6	...	46	10.7	-0.04
0.7	24.56	13.43	TECHNITROL TNL	0	...	43	1441	20.89	-0.43
1.3	38.65	22	TALBOTS TLB	0.4	1.3	16	2514	31.17	0.37
0.9	23.98	15	TXU TXU	0.5	2.1	dd	11914	23.93	0.06
0.7	24.56	13.43	TECHNITROL TNL	0	...	43	1441	20.89	-0.43
4	21.43	15.6	TAUBMANCtr TCO	1.08f	5	...	5840	21.42	0.16
14.4	21.78	8.31	TelNoCelu TCN	0	1.6	...	26720	22.06	0.34

YTD % CHG	YEAR HI	YEAR LO	STOCK SYM	DIV	YLD%	PE	VOL 100s	CLOSE	NET CHG
3.7	27.88	14.3	TEKNIP TKP	.90e	3.2	...	64	27.92	0.08
0.7	24.56	13.43	TECHNITROL TNL	0	...	43	1441	20.89	-0.43
4	21.43	15.6	TAUBMANCtr TCO	1.08f	5	...	5840	21.42	0.16
0.1	23.7	15.54	TJX Cos TJX	0.14	0.6	20	2918	22.08	0.11
0	22.09	10.6	TRC Cos TRR	0	...	29	410	21.06	0.06
2	29.99	12.09	TelNrdCelu TND	.46e	...	...	68	28.5	-0.5
-2	11.2	4.45	TelNoCelu TCN	0	1.6	...	46	10.7	-0.04
6.2	16.49	6.38	TelNoLeste TNE	.80e	...	...	13383	16.38	-0.11
-2.7	14.59	5.02	TelLeste TBE	0	1.1	...	50	13.5	0.05
0.1	23.7	15.54	TJX Cos TJX	0.14	0.6	20	2918	22.08	0.11
0	9.8	3.79	TV Acteca ADS TZA s	.75e	8.2	11	6898	9.1	-0.03
0.9	23.98	15	TXU TXU	0.5	2.1	dd	11914	23.93	0.06
6.6	12.93	5.89	TaiwanSemi TSM	stk	...	...	61438	10.92	0.01
1.2	1.2	1.2	TEKNIP TKP	1.2	1.2	1.2	1.2	1.2	1.2
3.7	27.88	14.3	TEKNIP TKP	.90e	3.2	...	64	27.92	0.08
0.7	24.56	13.43	TECHNITROL TNL	0	...	43	1441	20.89	-0.43
4	21.43	15.6	TAUBMANCtr TCO	1.08f	5	...	5840	21.42	0.16
0.6	52.25	36.5	TCF Fnl TCB	1.3	2.5	17	5921	51.66	0.59
1.7	73.4	32.4	TDK Cp ADS TDK	.45e	0.6	...	183	73.01	-0.39
0	9.8	3.79	TV Acteca ADS TZA s	.75e	8.2	11	6898	9.1	-0.03
0.9	23.98	15	TXU TXU	0.5	2.1	dd	11914	23.93	0.06
3.7	27.88	14.3	TEKNIP TKP	.90e	3.2	...	64	27.92	0.08
0	14.99	15.7	TelCeluSul TSU	.23e	0.5	...	247	14.35	-0.35
6.6	12.93	5.89	TaiwanSemi TSM	stk	...	...	61438	10.92	0.01
0.9	23.98	15	TXU TXU	0.5	2.1	dd	11914	23.93	0.06
-2.7	14.59	5.02	TelLeste TBE	0	1.1	...	50	13.5	0.05
2	29.99	12.09	TelNrdCelu TND	.46e	...	...	68	28.5	-0.5
-2	11.2	4.45	TelNoCelu TCN	0	1.6	...	46	10.7	-0.04
0.7	24.56	13.43	TECHNITROL TNL	0	...	43	1441	20.89	-0.43
1.3	38.65	22	TALBOTS TLB	0.4	1.3	16	2514	31.17	0.37
0.9	23.98	15	TXU TXU	0.5	2.1	dd	11914	23.93	0.06
0.7	24.56	13.43	TECHNITROL TNL	0	...	43	1441	20.89	-0.43
4	21.43	15.6	TAUBMANCtr TCO	1.08f	5	...	5840	21.42	0.16
14.4	21.78	8.31	TelNoCelu TCN	0	1.6	...	26720	22.06	0.34
1.2	1.2	1.2	TEKNIP TKP	1.2	1.2	1.2	1.2	1.2	1.2
-2.7	-2.7	-2.7	TECHNITROL TNL	-2.7	-2.7	-2.7	-2.7	-2.7	-2.7
4	4	4	TecoEngy TE	4	4	4	4	4	4
0.9	23.98	15	TXU TXU	0.5	2.1	dd	11914	23.93	0.06
6.6	12.93	5.89	TaiwanSemi TSM	stk	...	...	61438	10.92	0.01
3.7	27.88	14.3	TEKNIP TKP	.90e	3.2	...	64	27.92	0.08
0.7	24.56	13.43	TECHNITROL TNL	0	...	43	1441	20.89	-0.43
4	21.43	15.6	TAUBMANCtr TCO	1.08f	5	...	5840	21.42	0.16
8.3	19.1	10.45	TDC ADS TLD	.84e	4.3	...	60	19.66	0.61
0.6	52.25	36.5	TCF Fnl TCB	1.3	2.5	17	5921	51.66	0.59
1.7	73.4	32.4	TDK Cp ADS TDK	.45e	0.6	...	183	73.01	-0.39
0.1	23.7	15.54	TJX Cos TJX	0.14	0.6	20	2918	22.08	0.11
-2.7	14.59	5.02	TelLeste TBE	0	1.1	...	50	13.5	0.05
2	29.99	12.09	TelNrdCelu TND	.46e	...	...	68	28.5	-0.5
-2	11.2	4.45	TelNoCelu TCN	0	1.6	...	46	10.7	-0.04
6.2	16.49	6.38	TelNoLeste TNE	.80e	...	...	13383	16.38	-0.11
14.4	21.78	8.31	TelNoCelu TCN	0	1.6	...	26720	22.06	0.34
22.6	27.07	10.24	TelNoLeste TNE	.80e	...	...	40057	27.74	0.11
30.8	32.36	12.17	TelNoCelu TCN	0	1.6	...	53394	33.42	0.06
39	37.65	14.1	TelNoLeste TNE	.80e	...	...	66731	39.1	-0.03
47.2	42.94	16.03	TelNoCelu TCN	0	1.6	...	80068	44.78	0.06
55.4	48.23	17.96	TelNoLeste TNE	.80e	...	...	93405	50.46	0.01
63.6	53.52	19.89	TelNoCelu TCN	0	1.6	...	106742	56.14	0.37
71.8	58.81	21.82	TelNoLeste TNE	.80e	...	...	120079	61.82	0.06
80	64.1	23.75	TelNoCelu TCN	0	1.6	...	133416	67.5	0.01
88.2	69.39	25.68	TelNoLeste TNE	.80e	...	...	146753	73.18	0.08
96.4	74.68	27.61	TelNoCelu TCN	0	1.6	...	160090	78.86	-0.35
104.6	79.97	29.54	TelNoLeste TNE	.80e	...	...	173427	84.54	0.02
112.8	85.26	31.47	TelNoCelu TCN	0	1.6	...	186764	90.22	0.05
121	90.55	33.4	TelNoLeste TNE	.80e	...	...	200101	95.9	0.11
129.2	95.84	35.33	TelNoCelu TCN	0	1.6	...	213438	101.58	-0.03
137.4	101.13	37.26	TelNoLeste TNE	.80e	...	...	226775	107.26	0.06
145.6	106.42	39.19	TelNoCelu TCN	0	1.6	...	240112	112.94	0.01
153.8	111.71	41.12	TelNoLeste TNE	.80e	...	...	253449	118.62	0.06

Figure 2.3. Stock Pages

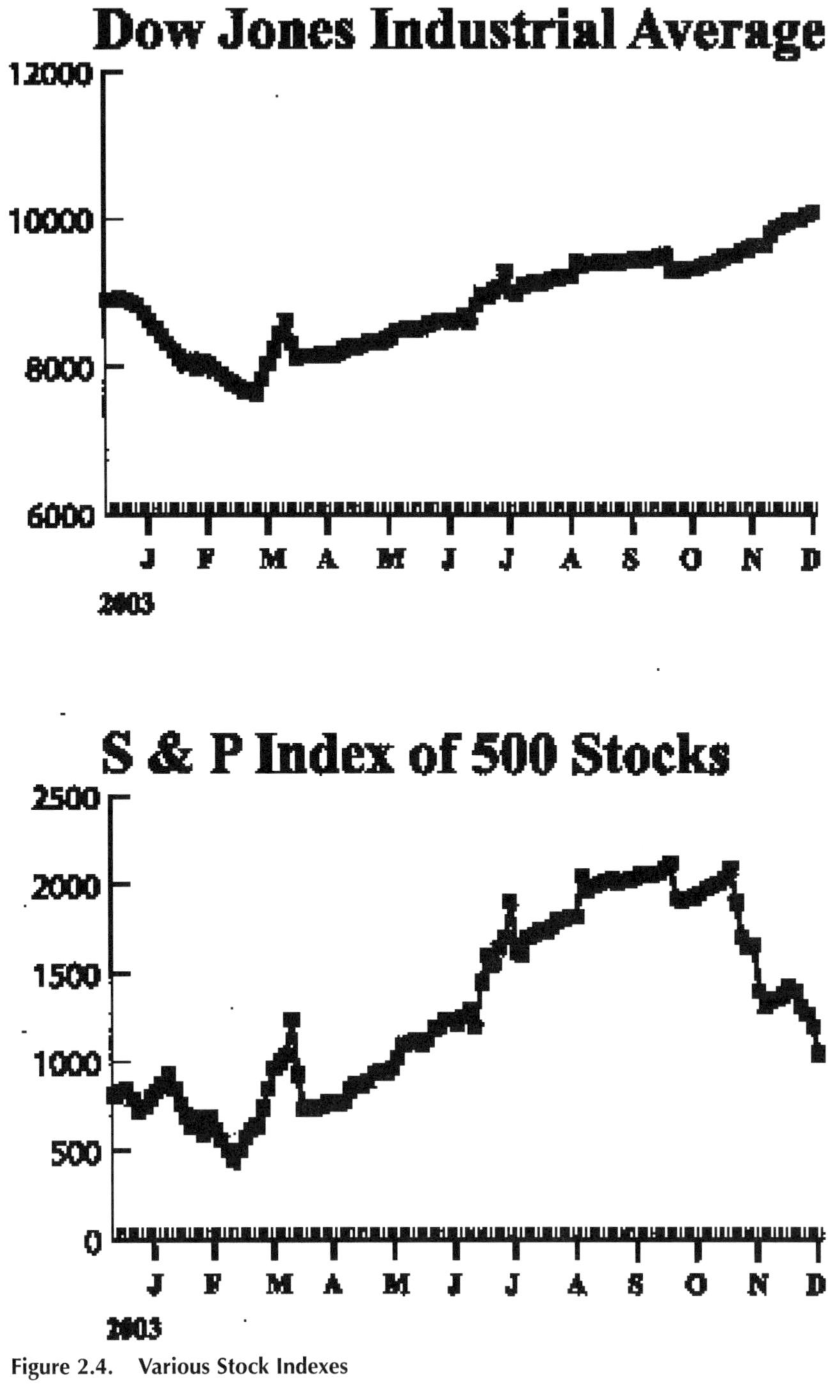

Figure 2.4. Various Stock Indexes

Dow Jones Average would increase or gain by 2 points. I have no idea why it is called the Dow Jones Average—pretty confusing stuff, but something to remember the next time a member of the public complains about the complexity of school data!)

The other index shown on figure 2.4 is, in fact, an index or composite of the net value of the included stocks for that given day. This report is a more useful tool than figure 2.3 (the listing of stocks) because it summarizes the stock data to a certain extent and shows relationships of value over time. It is also based on some analytics, albeit not as sophisticated as the prediction models used for the weather report.

CAN WE CREATE A SCHOOL WEATHER REPORT?

Unfortunately, the school analogy to the weather report—a single report that shows the various relationships between and among various data and one that predicts certain outcomes—simply does not exist today. As will be discussed in chapter 4, we may be able to run "root cause" analyses with school data looking for predictive relationships between and among input and outcome variables, but these analyses are very complex. Moreover, the graphical representations and output statistics are not easy to read or interpret. Regardless, our goal over the coming years should be to extract data, run these analyses, and present the results in an as easy-to-read format as the weather report to guide decision making.

Unfortunately, we more commonly provide data to teachers and administrators in the format similar to the stock pages—figure 2.3. Such reports are confusing and too unwieldy for busy professionals to make productive use of. Examples of this include item analyses by school, class, and student, which are often rather lengthy. There certainly is useful information here, but it is hard to sort out and make sense of.

Some testing agencies and state education departments are trying to provide information to districts in summary reports similar to those shown in figure 2.4; however, as we will see in chapter 3, these tend to be limited in what useful information they can provide because of the data aggregations used to create them. Other testing reports that take the detailed or individual student data by class and summarize it for teachers by learning objective are more useful. These are a good first step, but only that—more in-depth analyses are essential to reveal the changes necessary to improve achievement.

So, as we enter the twenty-first century, educators are deluged with data and information as they search for ways to summarize it, make sense of it, and look for trends and aberrations to help plan interventions. It would be wonderful if we had a report as informative as the school-data weather report, but it does not exist as yet. Until then, we are left to reports such as those represented in figure 2.4—roll-up reports of aggregate data. Subsequent chapters of this book will also describe useful school reports that take detailed data and chart it for interpretation.

WHAT QUESTIONS CAN BE ANSWERED?

Data-driven decision making is not a panacea or a crystal ball—it will not yield immediate and conclusive answers to your tough questions. The best it will probably do is guide your thinking, identify promising actions from a host of potential options, and help set your compass heading toward the promising intervention. As a result I am beginning to use the term "data-guided decision making."

A colleague asked me some time ago if I could help him identify which grant-funded program, among the many in his school district (an urban district where grants fund a large number of programs), had the most potential for improving achievement. It was a logical and important question, as he reasoned such information could assist him in focusing these otherwise disparate efforts. As I worked with his open-architecture database, I realized that we were not going to get an answer to his question because the district did not have adequate input and outcome data on each of these programs. If we cannot identify measurable variables as inputs and outcomes, then no useful analysis can be performed, even with the proper data-warehouse design. As we worked to get some of these data loaded into the system, time and frustration thwarted the effort. The basic problem was the district's inability to capture and load the needed data elements to do the basic analysis. I have witnessed this same problem repeatedly, which is why I included a section in this chapter on the messiness and incompleteness of school data.

This begs the question: If so many school improvement questions cannot be answered, why engage in data-driven decision making at all? What can be learned about student achievement in this environment? What queries can be run? And what can be learned?

This book explores the type, range, and scope of questions that can be addressed using data-driven decision-making techniques and tools. I am careful here to use the word *address,* not *answer,* because I have yet to find the discernible, irrefutable, incontestable answers to questions that lead to clear, actionable steps. Yet, everyone I know who works in this field would argue that the process is worth the effort because without it, one is left "shooting in the dark." Instead, this work helps to inform intuitions and guide decisions about what is working, what is not working, and what needs to change.

In general, the following queries are possible with the proper data loaded into an open-architecture or hybrid data warehouse:

1. Data disaggregation to find groups and subgroups of students not performing up to expectations or performing above expectations.
2. Longitudinal analyses to follow a specific cohort over time to determine if their growth is at expected levels.
3. Program evaluation (or at least initial efforts at program evaluation) to determine if course content and student achievement are meeting expectations of teachers, schools, and against state mastery tests or other standardized/criterion-referenced tests.
4. Cost-benefit analyses to determine if a program is working to expectations and is worthy of continued investment.
5. Root-cause analyses to determine which variables are predictors of some score or achievement variable.
6. Explorations that encompass many or all of the first five techniques to attain the more complex questions typically asked by school leaders. For example, a cost-benefit analysis of the reading recovery program would need to use root cause procedures, if possible, to try to isolate the reading recovery program as the key input variable. This analysis would likely require longitudinal techniques (because the analysis is done over time) as well as disaggregation techniques (since we need to know how this group did compared to the standard population). The more components of analysis we add, the more challenging the work becomes. Most of the questions asked require multiple strategies to answer.

DECONSTRUCTING YOUR QUERY

To explore the challenge of performing a query, let's look at a few examples of typical queries that school leaders ask. Here are a few that I have worked on with school principals and central office administrators:

1. Why do so many students perform below standard in math?
2. How do we determine what is needed to do well in reading and writing and how do we adequately measure progress toward that goal?
3. Does attending a high-quality preschool (for three- to five-year-olds) promote learning in elementary school? High school?
4. Is there a correlation between achievement levels on the eighth-grade reading mastery test and high school drop-out rates?
5. How many more students might graduate if poor attendance improved?
6. What is the correlation between participation in extracurricular activities and achievement?
7. Why didn't our fifth grade (or any grade) achieve its target set by the state for adequate yearly progress (AYP) under the No Child Left Behind legislation?
8. Does our reading recovery program work? Is it worth the investment?

To address these questions, ask yourself five questions:

1. What data do you need?
2. What query strategies are needed (e.g., disaggregation, longitudinal, root cause analysis, or several of these techniques)?
3. For each query strategy, what statistical analysis should be performed?
4. What other resources might be needed for #1 and #3?
5. Even with the proper resources, which questions are really answerable? Which are worth the cost-benefit of answering, especially if some questions require a lot of time and work on the part of your staff or a consultant to complete?

I have found that most educators' questions are searching for causality. These are questions that require the identification and isolation of some dependent variable, generally the achievement measure such as a test score, or drop-out rate, and a series of independent variables—the most likely factors that are causing the outcome. Of the example questions listed above, they could all fall into this general category, but questions #1, 2, 3, 5, 7, and 8 in the first list are clearly questions of causality at one level of sophistication or another.

One reason why this is such hard work is that it is often very difficult to assemble all the needed data into one database to do the analysis. You might be missing important data altogether (what if you did not capture all the students who attended each preschool—question #3?) or you may not have captured how long they attended each preschool, as it would be important to determine if time in attendance of the preschool mattered.

Now, assuming you had all or most of the data you needed, how would you go about doing this analysis? Questions of root cause require regression analysis, which is not a simple statistic to run and analyze. Even if you got this far, what are the results likely to tell you? When these analyses are run with a computer statistics program, a readout is generated of which input variables best predict the outcome for a given level of statistical probability. However, that level of statistical probability is not always convincing. Here we need to differentiate between statistical and practical significance. As you will see in chapter 4, statistically significant results are not always practically significant—at least not to a level that persuades you to take action.

LOOKING AT TRENDS—THE 3×3 MATRIX

To consider any finding practically significant—that is, one that leads you to take action toward change—you would want to know that this finding could be generalized beyond the "study" group of analyzed students. I have found that interventions are often warranted only when a convincing case is made after review of several cohorts of students (running the same analysis on each cohort). In general, a similar trend (or finding) across three cohorts, following each cohort over at least three years (in other words a 3×3 matrix), will often yield convincing results. However, because of "data messiness" issues, you will not always be able to replicate these analyses over the full 3×3 matrix, but you should certainly try for as many years as is practical.

So, a complex analysis in the first place becomes even more complex due to the need to search for trends across several cohorts. Because so many educators' questions inevitably end up being questions of causality, chapter 4 demonstrates what it takes to do this work, to search for these patterns, and what is knowable as a result.

EVEN SIMPLE QUESTIONS ARE NOT SO SIMPLE

What seem simple questions are often not so simple. Take, for example, question #4 from the list above: "Is there a correlation between achievement levels on the eighth-grade reading mastery test and high school drop-out rates?" The complication here is created by how a dropout rate is computed. Do you include students who reenter school after a year or two? What about those who go on to finish with a GED? After all, they may have spent a good deal of time in your school. What about those students who move out of town? How does your guidance office or attendance office code these students into your student information system in order to differentiate them from drop outs and students who left the school for other reasons? Do you have the date/time fields coded correctly so that you can dissagregate the different groups by date/time/periods?

Thus, to perform this analysis you will need to place each student into one of many groups; one group is composed of those students that graduate from your school and the other students need to be placed into as many groups as needed for the categories discussed above. Once you have all of this information in one database, it needs to be properly ordered into a spreadsheet program by group in order to run the correlation among the groups. Then you need to interpret the correlation—not an easy task given the inherent weakness of correlation as a statistic. When you are done with all of this work, you will need to repeat this entire exercise once or twice more to look for trends across a 3×3 matrix!

If that sounds like a huge task, it is, and it is why this is such hard, frustrating work for many busy and time-starved educators. A university scholar asked me recently, after hearing one of my presentations, "Isn't this just good, basic research?" The answer is—yes. And doing good, basic research is hard work.

SKILLS AND KNOWLEDGE NEEDED: SUMMARY OF THE NEW LITERACIES

Beyond the time and hard work needed to do this work, there is a set of discernible skills required for success. These are:

1. Knowledge of basic research skills, or the ability to deconstruct a question into a set of researchable steps.
2. Knowledge of your data—knowing the difference, for example, between the scale score and standard score on the mastery test or that algebra classes are coded differently (or the same) across schools.
3. Database skills—the ability to manipulate data in and out of databases to spreadsheet programs. This is necessary even with data warehousing systems because these systems will often require that you export the data into a spreadsheet for further analysis.
4. Knowledge of statistics (at least enough to know how to run and interpret correlations, to know when to use a t-test vs. an analysis of variance, and how to interpret the findings). Root-cause analysis requires a deeper knowledge of statistics.

It is rare to find all of these skills in one person; consequently, many school districts are tasking teams of individuals collectively holding these skills to work together on their most important queries.

SUMMARY

You must be wondering at this point whether this is all worth the effort. The answer is that we simply can no longer afford not to do this work—the pressures of accountability and the need to find practical teaching strategies and interventions are driving the field. Although *this is hard work*, the advances that school districts are making through data-driven decision-making techniques indicate that we are finally on the verge of identifying those interventions and strategies that truly impact achievement. This accomplishment alone makes the journey worth your time.

It is also clear that this will remain hard work for some time—the promise of a super technology is still a long way off. Our current technologies are allowing us to do this work more efficiently today than only a few years ago, but it still requires a good deal of time, effort, and skill.

After one of my presentations on this topic, I was asked if I thought we would eventually be able to engineer all of the steps for a complicated query into a computer program so all one had to do was ask the question. It would be like asking, "What is the impact of mobility on student achievement?" and the program would sort the right cohorts, make the needed matches, transform the data types to the required formats (as scores are generally not the same format from year to year nor have the same meaning even if they are the same type), run the needed analyses, and present and interpret the results. It was a serious question about the state of the art of data-driven decision-making practice and tools, and the everyday pressures of accountability school leaders face. You can imagine my answer given the content of this chapter!

Recently I was speaking with a colleague who had seen a presentation on web-based neural net data-mining technologies. The idea behind these technologies is to be able to ask a natural language question, and the program would then search the Internet and complete the needed analyses without any other input needed from the user. The question was: "What baseball games were played in the continental United States during May 2001 where the temperature was between 60 and 70 degrees Fahrenheit?" As my colleague relayed the story to me, the system went out to the Internet and found a list of all the baseball games played during that month, found out where they were played and the times of day, and then compared that information with the weather reports and yielded an answer to the user. I was intrigued with the story and wanted to find an application for school use. I'm sorry to report that, as of now, these technologies are just too expensive for our use—well north of hundreds of thousands of dollars for even a small school district. So much for applying this technology today!

There is a real trade-off in this field between the costs of these technologies, the kinds of questions you have about school improvement, and the time and effort you and your team need to invest to address those questions. As I said earlier, there is no weather report for school data yet invented that is affordable and solves all the data messiness problems associated with data-driven decision making. Maybe someday we will have these neural net technologies accessing our data warehouses, answering plain English questions. For now, however, we will have to invest a lot of effort to learn how to do this work.

Those who simply exhort educators to disaggregate data, run longitudinal analyses, or run root-cause analyses, without paying serious attention to the state of the art in data-driven decision making and the effort and knowledge that is needed, are doing the field, the public, and policy makers a serious disservice and injustice. Further, there are certain decision-support systems that advertise the ability to do these queries, but are really too limited to address your more challenging questions. This is why I urge you to make a list of your questions before acquiring one of these systems to be sure that, at a minimum, it has the capability of addressing your basic questions.

Thus, there is the real danger here of turning data-driven decision making into the next educational fad. Yet, the potential to have an important impact on achievement is real as these are the necessary techniques, when properly completed, that have been used to transform and improve private and public sector institutions for years. Thus, if we are to realize the promise of this work, a reasonable effort must be made to learn these new literacies and time must be allocated to get the work done.

NOTES

1. Software and Information Industry Association, *School Interoperability Framework*, www.sifinfo.org (accessed December 29, 2002).
2. Elliott Levine, "Building a Data Warehouse," *American School Board Journal* 189 (2002): 11, www.asbj.com/2002/11/1102technologyfocus2.htm (accessed December 27, 2002).
3. M. Parker, "Software options for data analysis," *The School Administrator* 58, no. 4 (2001): 8. Also available at: American Association of School Administrators, *Software for Data Use* (April 2001), www.aasa.org/publications/sa/2001_04/creighton_side_software.htm (accessed December 27, 2002).
4. P. W. Shorr, "Decision-Support Tools," *Scholastic Administrator* 3, no. 1 (2003): 41–46.
5. J. C. Wayman, S. Stringfield, and M. Yakimowski, *Software Enabling School Improvement through the Analysis of Student Data* (Baltimore, Md.: Johns Hopkins University Center on the Education of Students Placed At Risk, forthcoming).

Chapter Three

A Framework for Analyzing Your Questions

A good place to begin this discussion is with *your* questions about student achievement. Thus, I would like you to pause for a moment and answer the following question. It would be helpful if you could write down your response so that you can refer to it throughout this discussion.

Question: If you could get an answer to any question(s) you have about student achievement in your school or school district *today*, what would you like to know?

Please write down your response(s) here:
____
____
____

OK—you have a question. Now, the first serious issue to consider is whether your question(s) is answerable given the condition of your data and the resources needed to get an adequate answer. Many outstanding questions are just not answerable. Others can be given the proper approach and adequate resources. The purpose of this chapter is to help you make that determination.

A few years ago, we used to say that school administrators did not know how to ask the right questions. Frankly, we were dead wrong! My latest work indicates that great questions are typically asked, including tough questions about school improvement. The real problem is that most school leaders do not know how to deconstruct those questions into doable analyses, nor do they know how to run the analyses and interpret the findings. And even if they did know how to deconstruct the questions, run, and interpret the analyses, they often do not have the time since this is complex, time-consuming work. As a result, a good place to start is to determine how hard your question(s) is to answer and what it would take to get that answer.

A FRAMEWORK FOR YOUR QUESTION(S)

To guide you I will present a framework for (1) thinking about data-driven decision making, and (2) categorizing your question(s) in terms of its answerability and the level of effort it will take to get that answer. As mentioned earlier, I refer to this as a three-stage model of data-driven decision making. Briefly, Stage I uses aggregate data to compare institutions (such as how your school performed compared to others). Stage II uses detailed data (the individual students' responses) to determine what specific (content) areas and students contributed to your school's better (or worse) performance. Stage III gets at prediction and, to the extent possible, root cause, answering the question "why did you do better (or worse)?" As we go through this discussion, please think about the question(s) you wrote down and consider what it would take to answer it.

STAGE I—SEEING THE BIG PICTURE

It is impossible to work on every school achievement problem at once, so you need some way to determine where to start. Fortunately, almost every state in the nation has a website where you can explore Stage I questions. In some cases, these websites are produced by vendors who allow for comparisons across a wide range of data points between and among districts.

For example, the Standard and Poor's site for Pennsylvania and Michigan (www.ses.standardandpoors.com)[1] provides a great deal of information for both the public and educators to use in answering Stage I questions, such as: How does a district's achievement compare to other districts and/or schools on the state mastery test or Scholastic Achievement Test (SAT)? Does one school spend more than another? Is

Connecticut Mastery Test, Third Generation, % Meeting State Goal: The state goal was established with the advice and assistance of a cross section of Connecticut educators. Students scoring at or above the goal are capable of successfully performing appropriate tasks with minimal teacher assistance.

Connecticut Mastery Test, 3rd Gen. % Meeting State Goal		District 2001–01	District 2001–02	ERG 2001–02	State 2001–02
Grade 4	Reading	67	69	62	57.9
	Writing	72	70	64	61.2
	Mathematics	74	77	65	61.0
	All Three Tests	50.4	53.4	44.9	42.8
Grade 6	Reading	68	72	65	63.6
	Writing	64	70	62	60.0
	Mathematics	66	76	63	61.0
	All Three Tests	46.7	54.0	45.8	45.4
Grade 8	Reading	70	72	66	66.3
	Writing	63	60	58	58.8
	Mathematics	64	63	57	55.4
	All Three Tests	47.1	46.1	42.7	44.0
Participation Rate		97.3	96.9	97.2	95.0

Figure 3.1. Milford, Connecticut, Mastery Tests for 2001–2002

one district's pupil-to-teacher ratio lower/higher? And so on. The Standard and Poor's site is arguably the most comprehensive presentation and analysis of state school data in the country.

New York state's website[2] provides specific information on individual schools and districts and also provides for cross district and school comparisons, although the range of data points presented is far less comprehensive than Standard and Poor's.

For this section of the chapter, I will use Connecticut's site (www.cmtreports.com), as it will provide the basis for our exploration of a specific question I will pose shortly through the various stages of data-driven decision making.

Connecticut actually has two websites that one must look at to begin a Stage I review. One site allows you to review, in PDF format, the strategic school profiles by district or school provided by the Connecticut Department of Education.[3] The other (www.cmtreports.com) allows you to interactively change several variables to "drill-down" further in order to isolate achievement variables from a limited set presented.

To begin, we might explore publicly available information about Milford, Connecticut, using the strategic school profiles. The strategic school profiles present hundreds of data points, so let's focus in on the achievement

Connecticut Academic Performance Test, Second Generation, % Meeting State Goal: The state goal was established with the advice and assistance of a cross section of Connecticut educators. The goal represents a demanding level of achievement, which is reasonable to expect of students in the spring of their 10th grade year. Students receive certification of mastery for each area in which they meet or exceed the goal.

Conn. Academic Performance Test, 2nd Gen. % Grade 10 Meeting State Goal	District 2001–01	District 2001–02	ERG 2001–02	State 2001–02
Reading Across the Disciplines*	46	50	43	44.8
Writing Across the Disciplines*	56	63	52	51.0
Mathematics	50	48	42	44.1
Science	47	50	42	43.2
All Four Tests	24.3	24.9	20.9	23.7
Participation Rate	92.3	93.4	93	92.4

*Includes results based on an alternate form of the CAPT due to an adminstrative irregularity

Figure 3.2. Connecticut Academic Performance Test, Milford, CT, 2001–2002

data: Connecticut Mastery Test results in fourth, sixth, and eighth grades; the Connecticut Academic Performance Test (tenth-grade mastery); and the SAT results. Figure 3.1 shows a brief section of that strategic school profile.

We can see from the data presented that Milford, a district of about 8,000 students in Connecticut's "Educational Reference Group F" (primarily a wealth-based indicator used to group Connecticut districts from most wealthy "A" to least wealthy "I") did well compared to its peer ERG districts in the state. They also made improvements in almost all achievement areas from 2000–2001 to 2001–2002.

The district was equally successful in grade ten as shown in figure 3.2. This shows performance on the tenth grade Connecticut Academic Performance Test—an even more rigorous test than those used in fourth, sixth, and eighth grades.

Exploring the strategic school profiles further, we can see in figure 3.3 that Milford also performed better than its Educational Reference Group (similar districts) on the verbal SAT score, dropout rates, and percent of students pursuing higher education.

The overall picture for Milford looks good; they have made improvements over the past several years that have apparently resulted in improved achievement across the board, and whatever they are doing appears to be working better, overall, than their peer districts. However, we have no idea what specific interventions and groups of students may be contributing to their success from this Stage I review. Thus, if we do

SAT® 1: Reasoning Test	Class of 1996 District	Class of 2001 District	ERG	State
% of Graduates Tested	78.6	85.6	77.3	77.6
Mathematics: Average Score	471	482	497	503
Mathematics: % Scoring 600 or More	13.4	15.7	17.5	22.1
Verbal: Average Score	503	503	500	502
Verbal: % Scoring 600 or More	16.6	20.7	17.4	20.5

Dropout Rates	District	ERG	State
Cumulative Four-Year Rate for Class of 2001	8.4	10.7	11.2
2000–01 Annual Rate for Grades 9 through 12	2.3	2.6	3.0
1995–96 Annual Rate for Grades 9 through 12	3.3	4.1	4.6

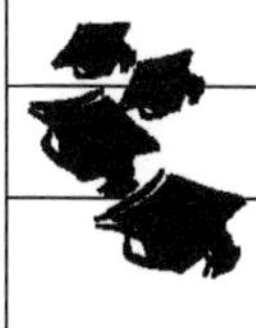

Activities of Graduates	Class of	# in District	District %	ERG%	State %
Pursuing Higher Education	2001	341	81.8	78.9	79.1
	1196	279	77.5	75.7	75.8
Employed or in Military	2001	44	10.6	17.5	17.1
	1996	59	16.4	17.98	18.7
Unemployed	2001	0	0.0	0.7	0.7
	1996	7	1.9	1.7	1.4

Figure 3.3. Milford SAT and Other Results 2001–2002

not know which interventions may be contributing to success or which students are doing well and which are not, the district will be unable to explore the *reasons* for their success more deeply. This, then, leads us to Stage II questions.

But before we go on, look at the question(s) you wrote at the beginning of this chapter. Are they Stage I questions? If so, you can probably go to your state's website and get an answer. However, I would bet that most of your questions do not fall into this category. If that is the case, then we go to Stage II.

STAGE II: WHAT SPECIFIC AREAS (AND WHICH STUDENTS) CONTRIBUTED TO OUR BETTER PERFORMANCE?

There are two fundamental approaches to exploring Stage II questions: (1) identifying the specific interventions, and (2) identifying what groups of students may be contributing to Milford's success. The first approach is to look at the data historically, or longitudinally, searching for patterns from

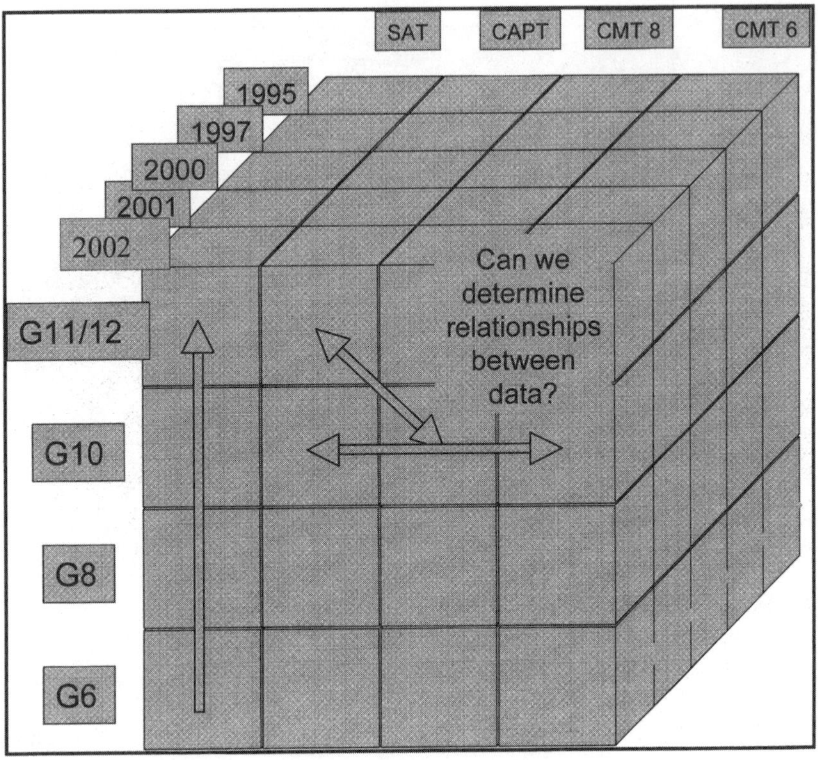

Figure 3.4. Longitudinal exploration of variables over time

fourth- to sixth- to eighth- to tenth-grade mastery results and on to SAT results in eleventh/twelfth grade. The second approach is to select out these same data, but disaggregate students by participation in program intervention. These two approaches are not mutually exclusive; they are iterative as we work to deconstruct the bigger question into doable analyses and proceed with the actual work.

The fundamental problem most districts run into at this point is that they do not have all of these data in one location or database. That is why more and more districts are investing in some form of decision-support system (DSS) and data warehouse. With a DSS-data warehouse, one can explore these issues in hours, not months. The complexity of these questions can be seen in figure 3.4 where I have graphically displayed the various interrelationships between and among each of these outcome measures.

What makes this an even more complex analysis is that each of these tests' outcome measures has several subtest scores. The SAT has a verbal and math component provided as a scale score between 200 and 800, while the tenth grade CAPT has several layers (various subject areas broken down by objective), as do the Connecticut Mastery Tests in grades four, six, and eight. And several score types are provided: raw, scale, and standard. For the CAPT alone, there are separate literature, math, science, writing, and reading scores, each with some level of subcomponents. For the fourth, sixth, and eighth grades, each learning area (reading, writing, and math) has several subscores, with math having as many as forty separate objectives measured (reported only as standard or ordinal scores). Each state's mastery test has similar levels of complexity. Figure 3.4 only

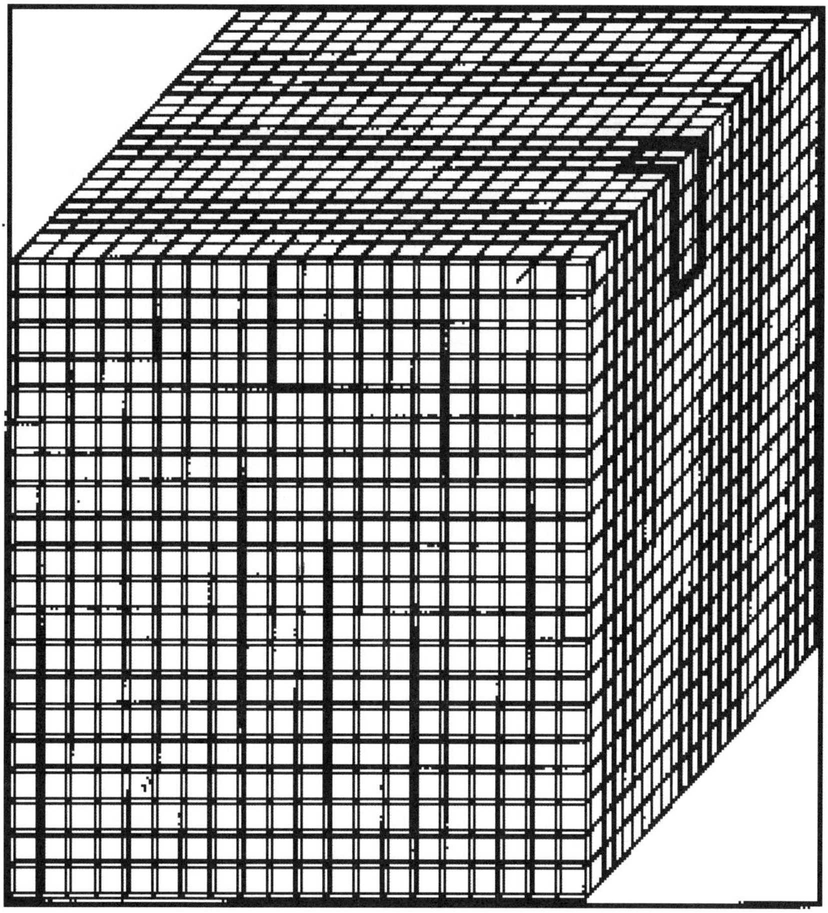

Figure 3.5. The full scope of the data variables

displays the top layer, but this can become very complex. The real picture can look more like what is shown in figure 3.5.

This is where decision-support and data-warehousing systems come in handy, as the system allows you to easily retrieve and analyze data from within this vast data set.

DECONSTRUCTING THE QUESTIONS

Let us now look more deeply at the second strategy or question I raised earlier: What groups of students may be contributing to Milford's success? The real issue here is how we can deconstruct this question into doable analyses; that is, what analyses should we run?

There are several options—some will be interesting but not particularly revealing, and others are truly interesting and revealing. Many educators might first ask what the relationship is between and among these variables—which is a question requiring correlation. We can also display the results of these analyses on a scattergram. Let's see what we can learn by running some of these analyses.

First, we need to get the required data that, fortunately in this case, resides in a database. Using Milford's data-warehousing system, I am going to select all of the relevant individual students' scores for the following longitudinal cohort:

- SAT 2002—eleventh grade
- CAPT 2001—tenth grade
- CMT—eighth grade 1998 (there is a three-year difference between the eighth grade and tenth-grade mastery tests in Connecticut because the eighth grade is a fall administration, while the tenth is a spring administration)
- CMT—sixth grade 1995

Once the data are selected in the data warehouse, I can export them to a spreadsheet program for further analysis. I use Microsoft Excel and import the Excel results to the Statistical Package for the Social Sciences (SPSS)—although some of this could be done directly in Excel.

[Note on running statistics: it should be clear by now that doing data-driven decision making requires some initial understanding of statistical operations. As we progress through Stage II to Stage III, the complexity of these statistics will grow. The question busy school leaders need to ask is, "How will I get this work done?" We are learning that there are three distinct skill sets needed for this work: (1) computer savvy (I define this as the ability to take a new computer program, load it into one's computer, and use it for a day or two without ever opening the program manual); (2) knowledge of your data (knowing that there are several scores reported on these mastery tests—scale, raw, standard, and the like, and knowing the difference between and among the various measures and tests); and (3) statistical knowledge (the ability to decide what statistics need to be run for the question under study, knowing what data are needed and the limits of those data, and knowing how to properly interpret the statistical results). We are also learning that these three skill sets are beyond the immediate grasp of most school leaders, so districts are typically tasking teams of individuals who collectively posses these skills to do this work.]

Let's start by performing a correlation. Figure 3.6 displays a sample of the correlation output from SPSS on these data. To keep this clear, I am only running a correlation on the key indices of math for each of the tests—not any of the subscores.

Correlations

		SAT_MATH	MATSCALE	MARWTOT8	MARWTOT6
SAT_MATH	Pearson Correlation	1	.829**	.763**	.742**
	Sig. (2-tailed)	.	.000	.000	.000
	N	212	211	206	210
MATSCALE	Pearson Correlation	.829**	1	.739**	.730**
	Sig. (2-tailed)	.000	.	.000	.000
	N	211	211	205	209
MARWTOT8	Pearson Correlation	.763**	.739**	1	.761**
	Sig. (2-tailed)	.000	.000	.	.000
	N	206	205	206	205
MARWTOT6	Pearson Correlation	.742**	.730**	.761**	1
	Sig. (2-tailed)	.000	.000	.000	.
	N	210	209	205	210

** Correlation is significant at the 0.01 level (2-tailed).

Figure 3.6. Correlation of Milford SAT 2002, CAPT 2001, CMT 8 1998, and CMT 1995 major learning areas

To begin, we can see that the correlation between SAT and the other scores are:

1. SAT-Math with MATHSCALE (tenth) == .829*
2. SAT-MATH with MARWTOT8 (eighth) == .763*
3. SAT-MATH with MARWTOT6 (sixth) == .742*

Each correlation denoted with an asterisk (*) indicates that the relationship between these two variables is statistically significant (shown also by the significance level of the "2-tailed t-test"). We are also presented with the number of students in each cell. While this is all very interesting, what is it actually telling us? What can be inferred? What decisions can be made?

Correlation is a statistical technique that tells us whether the two scores move in the same direction. In other words, the fact that the correlational value between the SAT-Math with MATHSCALE (tenth) is .829* tells us that there is a pretty good chance that if a student does well on the tenth-grade test, s/he also did well on the SAT. But the opposite could just as easily be true. In other words, if a student does poorly on one, they likely did poorly on the other. How often is this directionality accurate when looking at this particular correlational value of .829? To answer this question, we would square the correlation to find the percent chance that these values move together. In this case, the correlation is .829, so .829 multiplied by .829 is .687, or about 69 percent of the time (rounded off).

The issue now is this: Has any of this analysis so far answered my basic question of "what groups of students may be contributing to this success?" No! All we know at this point is that about one-half to two-thirds of the time (considering all correlations performed), students' scores move in the same direction as they progress from sixth to eighth to tenth to eleventh grade. So, while this might be interesting information, it reveals nothing to us about the key question we asked earlier.

Would displaying these results on a scattergram help? Let's see—figure 3.7 is a scattergram showing the SAT math score plotted against the tenth-grade mastery math test score (where the correlation above was the strongest).

Again, this is interesting, but not revealing very much in answer to my question. Here we can see how the scores "travel" together in certain directionality, but we do not yet have the specific information we are looking for.

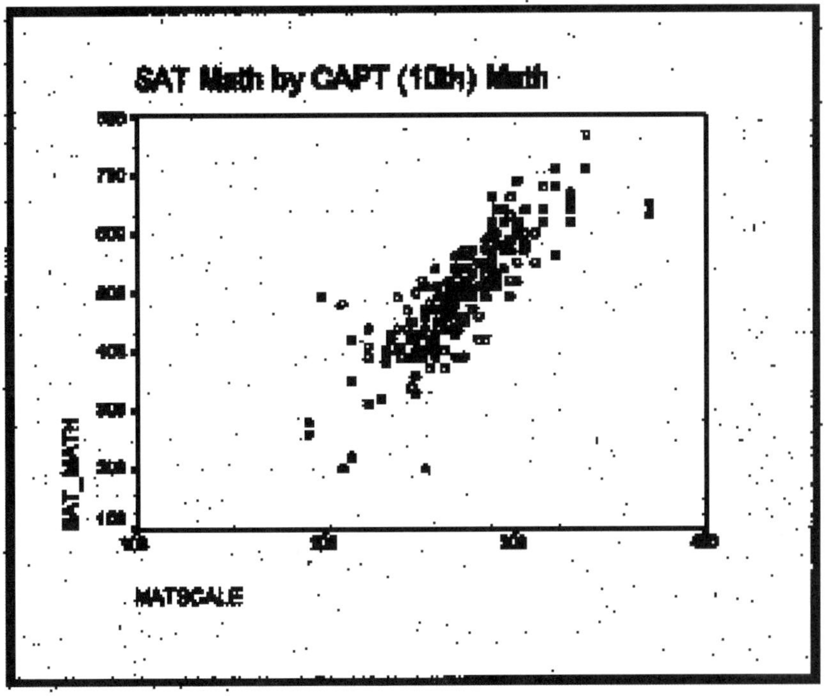

Figure 3.7. SAT Math 2002 by CAPT Math 2001

USING A DATA WAREHOUSE AND THE FILTER TOOL

Obviously we need another way to approach this question as correlation and scattergrams are not helpful. Again, the question is: What groups of students may be contributing to success? If we can answer this, we want to disaggregate these students by intervention to answer the second question: What specific interventions may be contributing to this success?

We need to define success first. The No Child Left Behind Act requires that each state set three levels of achievement proficiency that will be used to define success. Using this methodology, we can define success as:

- An increasing number of students moving from the lower levels of proficiency to the higher ones in any grade level; or
- A focus on one proficiency level—goal—and determining if more students reach that goal each year in a grade; or
- Following a specific cohort of students and determining if more of

CT Mastery Test Currently Administered in Grades 4, 6, 8 and 10

	YOG 2004	YOG 2003	YOG 2002
10th Mastery	2002	2001	2000
8th Mastery	1999	1998	1997
6th Mastery	1997	1996	1995
4th Mastery	1995	1994	1993

Figure 3.8. Cohort Models

"these same students" improve year to year (in other words, factor out mobility).

The first two definitions of success are easier to measure than the third because we do not have to follow a specific cohort of students over time, we simply need to know how each grade level does from year to year (fourth in 2002 to fourth in 2003, etc.). To address the first two definitions, we could simply use state reports, available often over the Internet, as discussed earlier in this chapter under Stage I. But the third definition is a lot harder to attain and requires special tools. It is also the answer school districts most want to know; that is, how students who have been in the district for several years perform over time. Let's focus on this problem because it will help answer my key question.

To know which groups of students are contributing to success in our Milford, Connecticut, example, we would need to have data covering cohorts for several years to select matching students. Figure 3.8 shows how this would work.

Figure 3.8 displays the necessary data sets to explore the longitudinal growth of each cohort of students by Year of Graduation (YOG). (Note that there is a three-year difference between the tenth and eighth mastery test even though they are given in eighth and tenth grades. This is because of the naming nomenclature used in Connecticut and because the eighth grade test is given in the fall, while the tenth is given in the spring—thus, a three-calendar-year difference in the naming conventions.) Earlier I spoke about the three skill levels needed for this work: computer savvy, knowing one's data, and statistical knowledge. This three-year difference between the eighth and tenth grade tests illustrates the need to "know" one's data.

To "know" which students contributed to Milford's success, we could use the model displayed in figure 3.8 and select specific students who were at a lower level of proficiency in sixth grade to distinguish which ones improved to a higher level of proficiency in eighth grade, and so on. Since No Child Left Behind will require that states set three proficiency levels, we could easily explore which students were at the mid level in sixth grade to see who improved to the higher level in eighth grade, and so on.

NOTE: I am unable to demonstrate the specific student results in Milford as doing so might unintentionally disclose the actual students. The same rationale applies to the establishment of minimum group size disclosure under No Child Left Behind—to maintain student anonymity. But to demonstrate how a decision-support system could work for the Milford example, the following data (figure 3.9) are contrived.

Decision support systems and data warehouses with ad hoc query capability can filter in and out specific data elements, which makes this query rather easy to run. In this case, we would set the filter to determine which students were at proficiency (level "2") in sixth grade (the mid level) and level "3" or higher in eighth grade (goal). This query result would display the names of students who met both of these conditions.

Using this technique, several queries could be run looking at the range of data contained in an example such as those in figure 3.8. Figure 3.9 shows an example of what might be retrieved, as again, this particular query result is fake data (see note above). Connecticut currently uses five levels of proficiency—with "4" being goal and "5" signifying advanced. The number 9 is used to denote a student who was absent for this particular subtest.

We can see that of the eight hypothetical students who scored low in sixth grade (Reading Standard = "2"), all improved (and one was absent

6th Grade Reading Standard Score to 8th Reading Standard Score			
5=Advanced; 4=Goal; 2 & 3 = lower levels of proficiency; 1=Intervention			
Grade Level	RD STD	Grade Level	RD STD
8	3	6	2
8	3	6	2
8	3	6	2
8	4	6	2
8	4	6	2
8	4	6	2
8	5	6	2
8	9	6	2

Figure 3.9. Contrived Data: Specific Students Called Up Using the Data Warehouse

from the eighth-grade test). The students who scored a "4" and "5" in eighth grade improved dramatically. Since all of these data would already be loaded into the data warehouse, we could continue to explore innumerable relationships such as this one. Using the ad hoc query capability we could also find out a lot more information about these individual students—what classes they took, who the teachers were, whether they received support, and so on.

For this example, I established a fake data set for one reading achievement cohort, but there are literally hundreds of data elements I could have used since reading, writing, and mathematics are broken down by objective and subobjective on these tests (which is true for most mastery tests used by states). Furthermore, I demonstrated this for only one cohort analysis, sixth to eighth grade. As figure 3.8 shows, there are many longitudinal relationships that could (and should) be run. Thus, if my data were real I would have answered, in part, the first question (at least for reading): "Which students are contributing to success?"

My second question was "What specific interventions may be contributing to this success?" Given the results shown in figure 3.9, we could query the database further to see what programs these students participated in during the two-year period. I could pull up their classes, special programs, special characteristics, etc., which is all very easy to do once you learn to use the ad hoc query tool. The assistant superintendent in Milford regularly runs queries such as this one and discusses the results with his administrative and teaching staff to determine what is working and what else they can do to improve achievement.

Due to the level of specificity of this analysis and discussion, Milford is making important progress and is one reason, albeit not the only reason, they are doing well compared to similar districts. Thus, through Stage II analysis, we can learn which specific students are contributing to success and begin to understand why they are doing well.

But this analysis cannot tell us which interventions actually *cause* that improvement—it only serves to identify possible relationships. While this might not seem like a huge difference, it is and this distinction is the subject of the next section.

STAGE III—KNOWLEDGE DISCOVERY AND ROOT CAUSE

When we ask questions such as, "What specific interventions may be contributing to this success?" we are really asking about causality or predictability. In other words, among the myriad of variables that might be contributing to success, we are asking which variables most cause that success. Another way of asking this is "Which intervention(s) can we count on to contribute to continuing success with new groups of students?" Thus, if we could, we would really like to know: "Which interventions *most* cause success?"—or, in other words, "What is the root cause?"

As I am writing this chapter, the United States has just experienced the shuttle *Columbia* tragedy as it was reentering the atmosphere on return to Cape Kennedy. There have been daily news briefings by the NASA shuttle manager, Ron Dittemore and others, as to what might have gone wrong. Throughout these briefings, Mr. Dittemore refers to NASA's search for the "root cause" of the accident—that single variable or incident that caused a chain reaction of events that led to the catastrophe. NASA focused on the foam insulation shed by the external tank, hitting the leading edge of *Columbia*'s left wing as *Columbia* roared into space. It is interesting to note how Dittemore refocused press questions on what might have led to that detachment (perhaps a basic design flaw in the external tank? or some other variable altogether?). On February 3, 2003, he made note of a "missing link" that he felt would lead to a better understanding of the "root cause" of the accident. During my revision of this chapter later that summer, the NASA focus shifted to the weakness of the leading edge tiles as the "root cause."

DEFINITION OF ROOT CAUSE

The best definition of *root cause* I have found is "a systematic process whereby the factors which contributed to an incident are identified."[4] There are many definitions, most focused on the engineering fields, but I prefer this one as it comes from the health-care field, which has many similarities to education in terms of the nature of our data and administrative systems. Root cause analysis is, therefore, the search for those factors that contributed—or caused—an incident, or, in our case, the improvement of achievement.

The key here is on the "systematic process" that helps to "identify" the cause. As we are about to see (in both this section and the next chapter devoted solely to this issue), root-cause analysis is not easy work and the tools are still hard to use and expensive, but my early work in this area is starting to illustrate that when we take the time to run a "systematic process," we can *begin* to isolate those factors that contribute to achievement improvements (or problems).

At this point, please pause a moment and take another look at the question(s) you posed at the beginning of this chapter to determine what stage of exploration and analysis is needed to answer it.

- Stage I uses aggregate data to compare institutions (such as, "how did our school do compared to others?").
- Stage II uses detailed data to determine what specific (content) areas and students contributed to improve (or worsen) performance.
- Stage III aims at prediction and, to the extent possible, root cause, answering "why did we do better (or worse)?"

If your question(s) asked about how your school/district performed compared to other schools and districts, then it is a Stage I question answerable using one of the statewide reports or websites. If you wanted to know how a group of students performed over time, whether one group did better than another (disaggregation by gender, race, etc.), what courses students took, who did well or poorly on an assessment, or whether students doing well on a state assessment also did well on related coursework, then these are examples of Stage II questions that require (1) the detailed student data and (2) some way to analyze those data with basic statistical operations. If your question in any way asked why something happened or whether you could use one variable to "predict" performance on another assessment, then you have asked a Stage III question.

Here are some examples of Stage III questions I have collected recently:

- Why do so many kids do poorly in math? (Examples: Grades, CMT/CAPT/SATs)
- How do we determine what is needed to do well in reading/writing and how do we "adequately" measure progress toward that goal?
- What are the most appropriate strategies for teaching reading/writing for special students and how do we measure that?
- Does attending a high quality early childhood program (three- to five-year-olds) promote learning in K–12?
- How many students would graduate if poor attendance issues improved?
- Is there a connection between fourth grade, eighth grade, and Math A exam scores (on state assessments)?

While these questions do not directly ask for root cause, they are questions of causality because they seek to identify how one or more variables affect another. The directionality of that question is what distinguishes it from Stage II. We learned in the Stage II discussion that correlation only tells us whether two variables are moving in the same direction, not whether one predicts another. For many of our questions, just "knowing" that students who scored well on the eighth-grade mastery test also scored well on the tenth-grade mastery test may be enough. But what if you want to know which earlier test scores, from the myriads available (see figure 3.8 and its related discussion), can be used to identify students at risk of performing poorly in the future in order to design and implement interventions? In this case, prediction analysis is required. The following example will demonstrate the cost-benefit of whether moving to the expense and complexity of

Stage III versus relying on Stage II analyses to address important questions is worthwhile.

EYEBALLING FOR CAUSALITY— BLASPHEMY OR REALITY?

Do you have to perform full-scale root-cause analysis (regression) to know if a program is working? Let's see.

Reading Recovery is an expensive program for districts—it requires the allocation of full-time equivalent teaching staff for very few children each year. The questions most superintendents ask are, "Does the program work?" and "Is it worth the investment?" A district I was working with recently asked this very question and, fortunately, they had loaded all the needed data into their data warehouse. They had lists of students who had participated in reading recovery when they were in first grade so that they could be tracked over time. Figure 3.10 displays the proxy results of one cohort analysis from 1992 to 2002. Again, these are contrived data mirroring the real results.

Figure 3.10 displays first graders who participated in Reading Recovery (RR) during the 1992–1993 school year and then shows their performance on the fourth, sixth, eighth, and tenth grade reading mastery tests (as measured by DRP unit reading scores). DRP goals in Connecticut are as follows: fourth = 50, sixth = 59, eighth = 64, and the tenth-grade reading test displays the standard score with goal = 4. The data show that in fourth grade several of the students are already above goal, having participated in Reading Recovery as first graders. By sixth grade, all but one student is at goal, with several considerably higher than goal. At eighth grade, *all* students are above goal with many well above goal. The tenth-grade test in Connecticut is particularly rigorous, more so than the fourth-, sixth-, or eighth-grade tests. To reach goal on the tenth-grade reading mastery test is quite an accomplishment, and we can see here that all but one student reached that goal. The one student who did not reach goal missed by one question for, as we dug deeper into the data, we saw that this student had a reading scale score just five points below what was needed for goal—on a scale score range of between 150 and 400. The question is: "Is the Reading Recovery program working and worth continued support and investment?"

Reading Recovery Students (GR1) for CAPT 2002, CMT 81999, CMT 6 1997 and CMT 4 1995				
10th RAD–STD	8thDRP–UNIT	6th DRP–UNIT	4th DRP–UNIT	1st Gr Year in RR
4	75.00	64.00	60.00	1992-1193
4	78.00	64.00	51.00	1992-1993
4	68.00	63.00	39.00	1992-1993
4	74.00	68.00	43.00	1992-1993
4	87.00	59.00	60.00	1992-1993
4	69.00	72.00	52.00	1992-1993
4	67.00	50.00	44.00	1992-1993
4	75.00	59.00	41.00	1992-1993
3	87.00	69.00	50.00	1992-1993

Figure 3.10. Contrived Data: Students Who Participated in Reading Recovery During the 1992–1993 School Year

This analysis looks convincing, but realistically one has to consider whether a host of other variables might have accounted for success on these tests after first grade. Maybe these kids had superior second- and third-grade teachers. That being the case, success could easily be the result of a combination of factors: participation in Reading Recovery and great teachers in the two subsequent years. Maybe the identification procedures/variables used to place them in Reading Recovery in the first place were flawed; that is, perhaps these students did not really need Reading Recovery. What other supports did these students have in grades two through ten? And so on—as we could develop a whole host of "threats to the validity" of my analysis. Some of these threats could be explored and eliminated from consideration, but most could not be adequately addressed to sway skeptics given the time and resources normally available. However, one thing we could do is to repeat this analysis over two or three more cohorts to see if this trend holds up. In this case, I did that further analysis, exploring the cohorts of 2000 and 2001. The result? The trend held up, showing that all students who participated in Reading Recovery over these three cohorts did very well through their academic career.

At the conclusion of this exercise, which took about an hour, I asked the superintendent whether he was going to retain the program. He said that the evidence looked compelling given the stated purpose of Reading Recovery—to accelerate students early in their education so that they can keep up academically. Thus, he decided to keep the program in place. While we did not have root-cause proof, we had persuasive evidence that the program is working. The cost benefit of attaining root-cause proof is probably not worth the added effort given all the inherent limitations of performing root-cause analysis. But, as we will see in the next chapter, when root-cause proof is needed, special tools and techniques can sometimes provide it.

Purists would argue this is not root-cause analysis—and they would be correct. Consequently, is drawing such a conclusion blasphemy? You will have to decide that for yourself but, given the level of work needed to obtain a more perfect analysis, I would be satisfied with the decision.

This Stage II analysis does not "prove" that Reading Recovery works or that participating in Reading Recovery predicts future success. What we can conclude from this analysis performed over three independent cohorts is that there appears to be a relationship between participating in Reading Recovery and later success in school. True, other factors can be at work here, and probably are. But exploration of the question at Stage II seems to indicate that the program should be retained. And, given this evidence, there is no cost benefit of going further.

This example used a 3×9 matrix to explore the problem. We used three cohorts of tenth graders (2000, 2001, and 2002) and looked back at their experience and performance when they were first graders—hence the 3×9 (three cohorts, each going back nine years). My experience indicates that when we explore trends over this length of time and observe commonalities, evidence so obtained can be both plausible and persuasive—even though we have not "proven" causality.

A graphical representation of the three-stage model I have presented in this chapter is displayed in figure 3.11

This chart shows the relationship between the complex tools and analysis techniques needed for tougher questions leading to root-cause analysis. It also shows that the more useful results are often obtained at the outer limits of this schema.

SUMMARY

We were wrong a few years ago when we said the problem with educators is that they do not know how to ask the right questions. In fact, they ask great questions. We now understand, however, that they have trouble deconstructing their questions into doable analyses, collecting and analyzing the needed data, and properly interpreting the results.

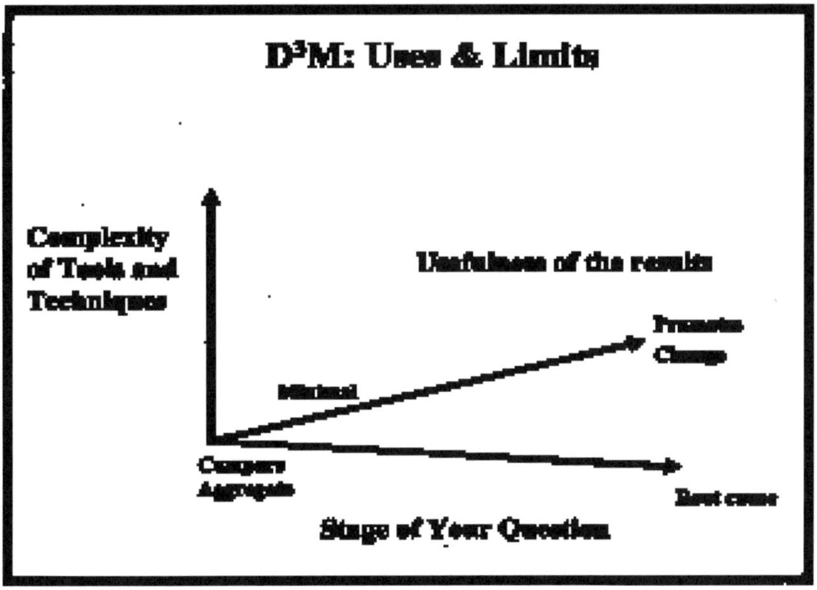

Figure 3.11. Data-Driven Decison Making: Uses and Limits

At the heart of the matter is the time required to do this work and the skills needed. This is complex work, demanding time to explore the relationships between and among data elements. The more important your key question is, the more variables you will want to consider.

Through this process, you are informing your intuition about what is going on, what is working, and what is not. Thus, you are guiding your decision making through the analysis of data. In this way, most of your important work can be accomplished using Stage II methods, assuming that the data are all collected and accessible in a decision-support system and data warehouse. Then, with enough time and skill, these questions can be explored.

Occasionally though, you need more proof or the variables are not as easy to "eyeball," as in the Reading Recovery case. For example, many districts would like to know which of the myriad of scores they have on a child going back to first grade are the best predictors of tenth grade performance. Dropout? SAT performance? College acceptance? And so on.

One superintendent asked his assistant to collaborate with me to identify what he termed the "key leading indicators" were of fourth-grade mastery results, since his district had loaded a wide range of early elementary data into their data warehouse. Questions such as these cannot be addressed through either Stage I or Stage II techniques. In this case, we need to address the superintendent's question through root-cause analysis, and the key challenge then becomes: "What is really knowable when we do this work?" Chapter 4 explores this question in depth.

Please go back and take a look at the question(s) you asked at the beginning of this chapter and ask yourself what stage that question falls into. What data are needed (aggregate or detailed)? Are the data accessible in electronic format? What steps are needed to answer your question(s)? What analyses will be needed? Who has the skills and time to do this work? What is the cost benefit of doing the analysis; that is, how important is the question? And what do you expect to learn as a result? If you answer these questions before you start your achievement-related question, you will be more likely to succeed in the end.

NOTES

1. Standard and Poor's, *School Evaluation Services*, www.ses.standardandpoors.com (accessed February 3, 2003).
2. New York State Department of Education, www.emsc.nysed.gov/repcrd/2002 (accessed February 3, 2003).
3. Connecticut Department of Education, *School Profiles*, www.csde.state.ct.us/public/der/ssp/index.htm (accessed February 3, 2002).
4. Australian Council for Safety and Quality in Healthcare, *Root Cause Analysis*, www.safetyandquality.org/definition/rootcauseanalysis.htm (accessed February 4, 2003).

Chapter Four

Finding Root Causes of Achievement—Can We Know?

Imagine being able to answer your Stage III questions regarding program effectiveness and causality accurately and precisely. Consider the value of determining the causes of poor achievement identified from one cohort and then scientifically applying that knowledge to predict students in subsequent cohorts who are at risk well before they reach that significant level of schooling.

To ground this discussion in your experience, please take a moment and revisit the question(s) you wrote down at the beginning of chapter 3—was it a Stage III question? If you have not had a chance to do that exercise, take a moment now and answer the following question. (It would be helpful if you could write down your response so that you can refer to it throughout this discussion.)

Question: If you could answer any question you have about student achievement in your school or school district today, what would you like to know?

Please write down your response(s) here:

____

____

____

In chapter 3, I presented a structure for thinking about your question(s)/problem(s). That structure, summarized, is as follows:

- Stage I: How did our school do compared to others?
- Stage II: What specific areas (and which students) contributed to our better performance?
- Stage III: Why did we do better? Can we predict?

If your question fits into Stage III, this chapter will demonstrate new technologies that will allow you to more effectively answer these questions. While these technologies are not ready for everyday use by practitioners—that is, they are not user friendly enough for your everyday use—this chapter will demonstrate the power of these emerging technologies. To reveal this software's capabilities, the last case study of this book (discussed in chapter 5) uses this technology to address one of my student's questions about finding best predictors of high school grade point averages (GPAs) from a host of earlier achievement measures with the purpose of being able to intervene much earlier in bettering a student's performance in high school.

More broadly speaking, I am often asked by school administrators if I can help them identify the important data from the bulk. I always ask, "What do you mean by 'really important'?" To which most respond, "The data that tell me if our programs work!" I have been working on that problem for years because I, too, wonder whether we could filter out all the extraneous noise from what really matters. In one case, as I mentioned earlier, a colleague asked a related question (his district was the recipient of several grants)—he wanted to know where to focus these resources so that they made the greatest impact. The common thread is that all of these questions demand root-cause analysis. That is, they seek answers to "Which of the data can predict outcomes?" And an even bigger question is, "What analysis is appropriate to attain this answer that would achieve findings that are reliable and valid?"

ROOT-CAUSE ANALYSIS

In science and technology, particularly engineering and medicine, root-cause analysis is a highly specialized field. It seeks to apply rigorous research methods and statistical analyses to identify "what is wrong" and "how to fix it." For example, with the recent outbreak of SARS around the world, the medical research community is hard at work to identify the source of the virus and how to stop it. As I write this chapter, NASA is focusing on weak leading-edge wing panels as the primary or root cause of the shuttle *Columbia* disaster. While we all know that small chunks of foam were shed from the large fuel tank on liftoff, contributing to the disaster, the foam was probably not the root cause—the weakness in the leading-edge panels are the likely cause. Recently (late summer 2003), NASA is under even greater scrutiny, not for the flaws in the hardware, but for their poor decision-making practices that may have led to the disaster. The larger problem may have been their failure to respond to the initial accident (it was first noticed in-flight) in a way that could have saved the astronauts' lives. In each of these cases, root cause is not apparent and requires deep analysis to complete.

The Holy Grail of educational research is to know what works in schools. And, until very recently, we could only tinker with the notion of finding the root causes of poor student achievement. There are student variables over which we have less control than others, such as poverty and the experiences children have before they first enter our schools. Beyond those—for the variables over which we do have control—what matters? Which best predict achievement in middle school? In high school? Which early interventions work best and under what conditions? Knowing the answers to these questions would allow appropriate intervention when we identify variables contributing to poor achievement. While chapter 6 will discuss the philosophical issues of what difference schools can make in our new accountability era, for now, let's focus on the statistical problem of "knowing" what matters within the context of available school variables, regardless of whether or not we agree on whether "knowing matters."

WHAT IS ROOT-CAUSE ANALYSIS?

Background

My interest in writing this book came about when I heard some educators speak nonchalantly about conducting root-cause analysis, as if it's something all of us should be able to do on an everyday basis. I had been working on the issue for some time, and I began to think I had missed the point, that somehow my approach was wrong. So I renewed my interest and revisited the definition and practice of root-cause analysis; how it worked and what it would take to achieve it. (All of this work is predicated on already possessing a data warehouse, making the process of accessing the needed data a fairly easy task). Thus, with access to several districts' data warehouses, I began to work on root-cause analysis around the questions school leaders were asking, such as: "What are the best predictors of mastery test achievement?" "Does the Reading Recovery program work?" "Is it worth the money we are spending?" and so on.

After several years of research into what it takes to "know" the answers to these questions with enough specificity to make a sound decision about educational programming (in other words, could I defend my decision to the teachers and parents affected and then to the Board of Education), I am ready to tell you that performing root-cause analysis is possible, but very difficult work. As a result, a theme of this book—avoiding the dangers of data-driven decision making—emerged through my research. There is danger in the belief that one can do this work quickly and easily. Sure, you can do a few quick trend analyses (as discussed in chapter 3) and maybe even draw some initial conclusions about possible causes, but these are likely to be of limited value in identifying actionable steps because these procedures lack statistical precision. Even the example I used in chapter 3, "Does Reading Recovery work?" was a laborious process to complete, and that was simple trend analysis, not the more sophisticated procedures I will discuss in this chapter.

Why use more sophisticated processes? As an example, I doubt you would want your personal physician using methods and medicines not fully tested and proven to work! In the realm of education, the good news is that, if you take the time to do this work properly with some of these new tools, then yes, a higher level of confidence in the analysis is possible.

There will be further limitations, however. Your analysis will likely be restricted by the available data and their inherent shortcomings (for example, the boundaries of what tests actually measure, the types of scores reported, and so on). To the extent we can do this work, it is highly specialized, using moderately expensive tools, and not yet ready for the mainstream. I expect that, over the next several years, researchers and vendors will find ways to commercialize these procedures, bringing them to the field at large. But for now, my purpose in this chapter is to demonstrate (1) that this work is possible, (2) what it takes to do the work, and (3) that root-cause analysis as currently practiced by the field today is more fad than science.

The Challenge of NCLB and the Potential of Rule-Based Decision Making

Schools are dealing with greater accountability pressures today than we have seen in recent memory. The fundamental goal of the federal No Child Left Behind act (NCLB) is to hold schools accountable for student achievement, prompting them to review test scores so that effective interventions can be designed for underperforming schools (and low-achieving students). Thus, the goal should be to identify successful interventions that promote improved achievement. This can be accomplished using root-cause analysis to determine the predictors of achievement, or key indicators (e.g., which programs work, what variables best predict successor achievement, and so on) and then ascertain whether those indicators hold true for the next cohort, and the next, and so on.

This last point is critical and is what sets this work apart from all other issues previously discussed in this book. In chapter 3 I demonstrated how trend analysis over a 3×3 matrix can be used to intuit that a program is working, but I made the point that this level of analysis yields little more than an educated guess, an educated intuition. Now I would like to add statistical precision to this problem.

You might be thinking: Why not just run regression analyses? You would be partially correct. Traditionally we have used regression analysis to determine the best predictors of some outcome variable. For example, if I wanted to determine which variables from the fourth-, sixth-, and eighth-grade mastery tests best predict tenth-grade science mastery test scores (where there is no science measure in fourth, sixth, or eighth grade), I could use regression analysis to find the set of variables that "best predict" that tenth-grade science score. But that would be it; I could not apply this knowledge with any statistical precision to the next cohort (2001), or the next (2002), and so on. Thus, at this point I am back to presuming that what mattered for the cohort of 2000 also applies to the cohorts from 2001 and 2002.

This chapter is about going the next step or knowing with statistical precision that the set of variables found for the first cohort also applies to subsequent cohorts. This is what is referred to as rule-based decision making, where a rule that is determined as applicable to one cohort can then be applied to another. The analog here is medicine. If I present certain symptoms to my physician, he will be able to recognize my illness and prescribe a regimen because the symptoms meet the same criteria as ones that have been identified previously through specialized trial studies.

A key assumption in the federal No Child Left Behind law is that educators posses the tools and abilities to identify these leading "key indicators" that will make a difference in student achievement. Current data-analysis techniques used in data-driven decision making, however, limit us to looking back in time: "How did this cohort of students perform and what were their predictors of performance?" Educators are then left to make potentially erroneous assumptions that the predictors of a particular cohort will hold true for subsequent cohorts. While this may turn out to be the case, there has been no way to systematically prove it, in other words, to prove that a "finding of fact" or "root cause" identified for one cohort can be applied with confidence to subsequent cohorts. If such a system could be devised, the potential success of school interventions could be greatly enhanced and the nation would have a better chance of meeting NCLB's lofty goals.

New Artificial Intelligence Tools

New techniques in data mining and Artificial Intelligence (AI) now provide the tools to develop a predictive model developed from a current or past cohort that can be applied to subsequent/future cohorts to predict their performance more accurately. These predictive models will allow for the identification of leading indicators to develop effective interventions for improving student achievement. To the extent that prediction analyses can be considered findings of fact (or the identification of root cause from the variables studied), these new techniques can provide crucial answers to the question of "what works in schools?"

Over the past several years, I have been experimenting with tools and techniques that might prove successful in this work. While I know of a few tools that can get the job done, they are extremely expensive and out of reach for schools. Thus, I was left to work with the ones that are affordable—a key principle that I hold to in my work. (It does not make sense to work with tools that are unattainable for the field at large.) However, to my chagrin, none of those efforts proved very successful. What appeared to work on one cohort could not be reliably duplicated on another. While one technology would work on certain data types, it would not work with others (because of a mix of variables types, such as combining scale scores with ordinal scores).

These early attempts did not work principally because I was using tools that limited me to looking back in time—i.e., how did this cohort perform and what were the leading indicators of their achievement? But when I tried to apply that knowledge to a second cohort and a third, I could not find any persuasive (valid and reliable) trends across cohorts. Thus, I was unable to develop a systematic way to apply the knowledge learned from one cohort to another in the same school or school district. This is due to the fact that traditional regression methods enable one to find which variables best predict an outcome for a particular cohort, but there is no way to systematically apply that knowledge to a subsequent cohort. Having reported on these attempts over the past several years at various conferences and in papers, I ended my work about a year ago in a fit of frustration. The problem is further compounded by a lack of educational literature on this topic.

Then I recently learned of new advancements in Artificial Intelligence and data mining that might lead to success. Most of these new tools are very expensive, well beyond the financial resources of educators. As noted above, one of the concepts I have held onto through all my work is that whatever we do, it must be affordable. While the new toolset I report on here is not a shrink-wrap (a few hundred dollar) application, it is a lot less expensive than anything else I have seen on the market. Of course, it requires that you already have a relational database or data warehouse and the skills necessary to run the software, which are necessities beyond most of us, but this will improve in time. The price for the data mining software alone (at the time I am writing this—late Spring 2003) is around $22,000. That does not include the development of the data warehouse or the human resource time necessary to learn the toolset. This might sound expensive, however, this application is a lot less costly than the others I reviewed, literally a fraction of the cost of another well-known toolset in this space, and it works with educational data on the questions school leaders most want to know. The toolset is modular, that is, you only need purchase the algorithms you desire. And my early work with it indicates that educators might simply need the base system plus a couple of the twelve algorithms that comprise the total toolset. If this turns out to be true, then that $22,000 figure can be reduced substantially.

We are still a long way from taking this toolset, or ones like it, and weaving it into the everyday fabric of school decision-making applications, but we are now on the way. The purpose of the remainder of the chapter is to demonstrate what can be done with these technologies. Over the coming months and years, I expect to find ways to make this technology more accessible and useful. But, for now, this is what it takes to do root-cause analysis.

PILOT STUDY WITH ARTIFICIAL INTELLIGENCE AND RULE-BASED DECISION MAKING[1]

To explain what this new technology is capable of, the following pages report on a pilot study I conducted using this software. The study was performed across four Connecticut school districts, one urban and three suburban, where a new Artificial Intelligence tool was used on each district's data to accurately develop a rule-set from one cohort's data that was then applied to predict outcomes for subsequent cohorts. The advent of these technologies raises the potential of providing educators important and useful information about where to focus their intervention resources in the pursuit of improving student achievement.

RULE-BASED DECISION MAKING

Rule-based decision making (coupled with data-mining techniques) has been used in the private sector to identify important trends and key predictors of outcomes in the retail, manufacturing, and governmental sectors. (Note:

data mining as used here is the classic definition, utilizing prediction analyses, not how it is often used in education, parochially, to describe the basic review of performance trends in many of the writings on data-driven decision making.)

New advancements in Artificial Intelligence software have made these technologies accessible to educational researchers because (1) the cost is coming down and (2) these programs can now more easily "connect" to existing school data warehouses. These tools are being used in the private sector to identify root causes of specified outcomes (dependent variables) with new speed, efficiency, and accuracy.

I used Megaputer's PolyAnalyst® computer program to identify leading indicators in the pilot study reported in this chapter.[2] The winner of several awards in the AI field, PolyAnalyst® develops a rule-set, or predictive model based on a particular cohort's data and then that rule-set can be applied to a subsequent cohort's data to accurately predict their same dependent variable. Prior to the advent of this technology, we had been able to determine predictors of achievement using classic regression methods, but we had not been able to transform that knowledge into a statistically reliable rule-set for application to another cohort's data to predict their outcome variable. This is a new and exciting development in Artificial Intelligence that could greatly assist school leaders in understanding what interventions work and what interventions are needed early-on in a child's educational career to make a difference in their learning.

Writing on the topic of rule-based systems, Dhar and Stein note that "rule-based systems are programs that use preprogrammed knowledge to solve problems. . . . You can view much of problem solving as consisting of rules, from the common sense 'If it's warm, lower the temperature' to the technical 'If the patient appears to have pallor, then he must have an excess of bilirubin in his blood or be in shock; and if there's an excess of bilirubin in the blood, then administer drugs to lower it.' . . . Of all the situations you can think of, whether they involve planning, diagnosis, data interpretation, optimization, or social behavior, many can be expressed in terms of rules. It is not surprising, then, that for several decades rules have served as a fundamental knowledge representation scheme in Artificial Intelligence."[3]

While my pilot study did not follow the exact steps and processes of classic rule-based decision making as outlined by Dhar and Stein, the same concepts apply in that I am identifying a set of predictive indices that, taken together, form a rule-set or model that can be used to predict the future achievement of subsequent cohorts accurately.

MEGAPUTER POLYANALYST® 4.5

Of the new Artificial Intelligence technologies designed for this work, Megaputer's PolyAnalyst® was chosen because it is powerful and relatively inexpensive compared to others on the market. Equally important, PolyAnalyst® employs several advanced Artificial Intelligence data-mining algorithms applicable to the student performance challenge posed by No Child Left Behind. Following is a description of PolyAnalyst® by Megaputer:

> PolyAnalyst is a next-generation data mining system. Data mining represents a new and promising branch of Artificial Intelligence (AI) that embraces different technologies aimed at the automated extraction of knowledge (meaningful patterns and rules) from databases (large amounts of raw data). For a long time, knowledge acquisition has been the bottleneck in the process of turning the raw data into informed and successful business decisions. That is why data mining is the hottest AI application today—gradually, more and more people understand the necessity and advantages of using machine learning methods for intelligent data analysis. The goal of data mining for a company is frequently to improve profitability through a better understanding of its customers, sales, products, or operations. However, data mining is not restricted to marketing and business—finding patterns and rules in raw data can be important to science, medicine, academia, and engineering as well. The growing amount of information available from computerized storage and the increasing complexity of this information make it impossible for a human to come up with an effective solution. This makes data mining the technology of the future for every profession. One of the most advanced exploration engines, *Find Laws*, utilizes our unique *Symbolic Knowledge Acquisition Technology*™ (SKAT)—a next-generation data mining technique. PolyAnalyst automatically finds dependencies and laws hidden in data,

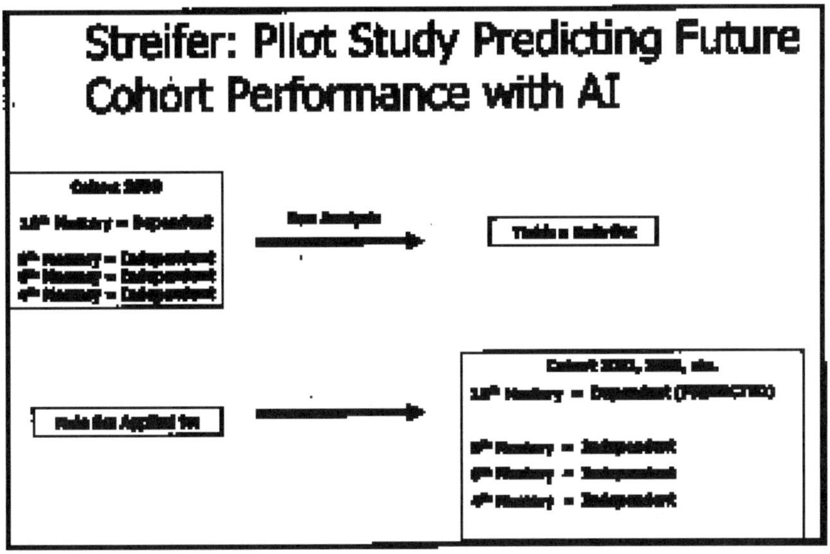

Figure 4.1. Pilot Study Design

presenting them explicitly in the form of rules and algorithms. The system builds empirical models of an investigated object or phenomenon based on the raw data. The user does not have to provide the system with any assumptions about the form of the dependencies—PolyAnalyst discovers the hidden laws automatically, regardless of how complex they are.[4]

THE PILOT STUDY

The purpose of the pilot study was to determine if a rule-set, or predictive model, could be developed that would help identify students early in their education who might be at risk of poor achievement several years later and to identify which variables, among the many available, could be used to design effective interventions. The pilot was also designed around the reporting requirements set forth in No Child Left Behind. The scope of this pilot study was a test of the technology to develop the rule-set and then to test that rule-set's accuracy when applied to subsequent cohorts in the same school district. If we can have confidence in the rule-set, we can accurately predict students' achievement in later grade levels well before they reach that stage of their education.

This pilot study was conducted on four Connecticut school districts' achievement data that were already loaded into a robust data warehouse containing a great deal of historical data on each student. A typical data warehouse, which forms the basis for extracting the data needed for these analyses, would house several hundred data variables on each student for each year that they are in school. Some of these data warehouses contain historical data dating back ten, even twenty, years. Mining these data warehouses becomes a virtually impossible task without the proper technologies. For this pilot study, tightly aligned state mastery test scores were used to determine the usefulness of the Find Laws data-mining algorithm in PolyAnalyst® to predict a selected dependent variable. A graphical representation of the study is shown in figure 4.1.

For each district in the pilot study, the baseline cohort from 2000 was selected as either tenth or eleventh graders (for selection of the dependent variable) and several earlier test scores were then used as potential predictors (independent variables). A rule-set was developed using the PolyAnalyst® Find Laws algorithm that was then applied to one or more subsequent cohorts (2001 and 2002). Since I already knew the actual dependent variable from 2001 and 2002, I could test the accuracy of the Find Laws rule-set in predicting the dependent variable.

What does a rule-set look like? Here is a very simple rule-set developed by PolyAnalyst:

SCI_STD=(−1.8002 *DRP_RAW8+2.33305 *MA_11_6+196.441)/
(1−0.0102987 *DRP_RAW8)

The computer program has determined that the DRP (degrees of reading power) score from eighth grade and the eleventh-grade objective level score of the math subtest from the sixth grade are the best predictors of tenth-grade science mastery score. The computer identified these predictors from the many that I used as independent variables. The rule-set is in the form of an algebraic equation, although not fully intended to be one. It is represented as a symbolic language that is interpretable by the user so as to identify the predictor variables. You cannot take this formula and directly apply it to the subsequent cohort data set in a spreadsheet program; this must be done by the Megaputer PolyAnalyst® software itself. But this symbolic language is very useful in allowing us to see "inside the black box" that is normally hidden to identify which variables matter most.

The rule-set above is a straightforward one. Here is a better example of what most of them look like, at least the ones I encountered during my pilot study:

Best significant rule found:

```
MAT_STD = (48.5639 *MA_CON_RAW8 *MA_PRO_RAW8*if
  (−0.00716027 <=
1/MA_PRO_RAW6 and 1/MA_PRO_RAW6 <−0.00716027 +
0.0347716 ,1/LA_WC_RAW8,0.049486)−0.104334
*MA_CON_RAW8*MA_PRO_RAW8*MA_PRO_RAW6+4.14677
*MA_CON_RAW8*MA_PRO_RAW8-0.028223
*MA_CON_RAW8*MA_PRO_RAW8*MA_PRO_RAW8+4978.8)/
  (MA_  CON_RAW8
*MA_PRO_RAW8+1316.62)
```

A word or two on the statistics reported here. Regression models provide many detailed and complicated statistics to help interpret the value of the outcome in the form of output/information. Since this is not a research paper, I have decided to provide only the critically important information to help interpret the results of the pilot study. Among the output provided, regression models are typically expressed in terms of the percent of variance explained by the prediction model that in turn is expressed by the value R^2. An R^2 over .4 is generally acceptable as a worthy research outcome, with an R^2 greater than .6 being very strong. Many of the R^2 values (outcomes) of this pilot study were in the ranges of .5 and .6.

I also used two other statistical procedures to test the accuracy of the predicted variable (by the PolyAnalyst® rule-set) against the actual variable from the subsequent cohorts—correlation and paired-samples t-test. Here I wanted to know how well the "predicted" outcome (or dependent variable) mirrored the actual outcome from the subsequent cohorts.

The first way I did this was to run a correlation between the predicted and actual scores expressed as a Pearson R correlation value. A Pearson R of .4 or greater is generally viewed as an acceptable positive correlation, but we really want to see these values higher than .4. Most of the correlations in this pilot study were .6 or higher—with many at .7 or even .8. What this means is that there is a very positive relationship between the actual score and the predicted score or, as discussed in chapter 3, the scores move together: if the score on one variable is higher, it tends to be higher on the other, too and vice versa.

The final statistic I ran was a paired-samples t-test between these same two scores (predicted vs. actual). The t-test is a more powerful statistic than correlation and it is used to determine if there is a statistically significant difference between two matched sets of data such as a pre- and post-test. For my purposes, if the prediction model or rule-set worked, then I would expect no statistical difference between the two sets of scores. As you will see, this was not always the case, meaning we are not ready to declare victory over root-cause analysis quite yet! (I will discuss this more fully later along with some of the potential reasons why this occurred.) Finally, I have left out all the other statistics and output that normally accompany these analyses and will report on those in other publications.

There are several good references on statistical analysis for educational applications that you may want to read on the topic to gain a more in-depth knowledge if statistics is not your strong suit, including Berk and Carey,[5] Carroll and Carroll,[6] Creighton,[7] and Utts[8] among others.

PILOT STUDY RESULTS

The results of the pilot study were encouraging with the R^2 of the prediction models ranging from .260 to .625, with the majority greater than .450. For the analyses yielding higher R^2 values, we have confidence that the rule-set works to predict the outcomes in subsequent cohorts. To test this assumption, correlations were performed between the actual outcome variable and the predicted outcome variable for the cohorts of 2001 and 2002 since the actual values were known. Correlations (Pearson R) ranged from .466 to .812, with most greater than .600. As a final test of the assumption, paired-samples t-tests were performed between the actual and predicted outcome variables, expecting that there would be no significant difference between matched pairs. This held true in most cases, but not in all as some of the rule-sets yielded outliers. This raises a series of follow-up questions that I discuss later, such as whether additional and different variables could result in a better rule-set. There are also problems associated with colinearity not addressed here.

The pilot study was first performed on three suburban districts' data that then led to a more robust test of the technology with an urban database.

DISTRICT CHARACTERISTICS AND VARIABLES STUDIES

Suburban District 1:

(Approximately 5,000 students, suburban/urban mix) The dependent variable was the Connecticut tenth-grade state mastery test in science (scale core). The independent variables included several that the district felt would be useful in this analysis from their sixth- and eighth-grade state mastery tests (and a mix of score types from raw to scale to ordinal). The rule-set developed from the 2000 cohort data was then applied to the same tenth-grade cohort data from 2001 and 2002.

Suburban District 2:

(Approximately 8,000 students, suburban/urban mix) The dependent variable was the Connecticut tenth-grade state mastery test standard score in math. For the purposes of NCLB, students' raw and scale score data are rolled up into categories to determine if a school is meeting standards. Connecticut and many other states have been using these standard score breakdowns for some time as a way of reporting state mastery test results. I was interested in verifying if the standard scores (which should be considered ordinal variables not normally used in prediction modeling) could be used exclusively in the Find Laws algorithm. (According to Megaputer, PolyAnalyst® is designed for such analysis, but I must admit I was skeptical since I had previously used other software that also purported to work with ordinal data and did not for a variety of reasons.) Thus, the independent variables used for this district were the standard scores achieved by each of the students on the 36 to 40 separate math objective standard scores from the sixth- and eighth-grade mastery tests. The rule-set developed on the 2000 cohort data was then applied to the same data from 2001 and 2002 cohorts.

Suburban District 3:

(Approximately 4,000 students, suburban, high performance) The dependent variable in this case was the eleventh-grade Scholastic Achievement Test (SAT) verbal scale score. Here I was interested in determining if state mastery test data could be used to predict SAT achievement. The independent variables included all of the raw or scale score data on Connecticut mastery language arts subtests from fourth, sixth, and eighth grade (opting for scale scores where available). This district was missing some data that prohibited the predictive model to be applied to the cohort of 2002, thus it was only applied to 2001. The predictive model could have been modified to include only those variables existing across all three cohorts, however, that step was not taken in this pilot study.

Urban District:

(Approximately 20,0000 students, urban) Following these three successful software runs in suburban settings, I decided to try a more robust exercise on an urban district's data. The dependent variables selected for the pilot study included the Connecticut tenth-grade state mastery test standard scores in science, math, and language arts. The independent variables included all of the available raw/scale scores (not duplication on a subtest; I took the best available score—raw or scale) on major subtests from the state mastery test in fourth, sixth, and eighth grades in math, language arts, and writing. The rule-set developed on the 2000 cohort data was then applied to the same data from the 2001 and 2002 cohorts.

Table 4.1. Find Laws Data Model Results

CITY SCHOOL DISTRICT Predicted Variable	*10th Science*	*10th Math*	*10th Lang/Read*
Cohort 1 (2000) Find Laws			
Data-Mining Model R^2	0.500	0.630	0.260
Predicted Cohort 1 (2001)			
Pearson R: actual vs. predicted	0.739	0.845	0.639
Paired Samples T-test p value	0.091	0.000	0.000
Predicted Cohort 2 (2002)			
Pearson R: actual vs. predicted	0.711	0.741	0.640
Paired Samples T-test p value	0.786	0.000	0.030

Table 4.2. Find Laws Data Model Results

District *Predicted Variable*	*Suburb 1* *10th Science*	*Suburb 2* *10th Math*	*Suburb 3* *SAT Verbal*
Cohort 1 (2000) Find Laws			
Data-Mining Model R^2	0.453	0.540	0.625
Predicted Cohort 2 (2001)			
Pearson R: actual vs. predicted	0.719	0.661	0.812
Paired Samples T-test p value	0.998	0.001	0.000
Predicted Cohort 3 (2002)			
Pearson R: actual vs. predicted	0.596	0.466	
Paired Samples T-test p value	0.348	0.013	

For each district in the pilot study, several pieces of information are provided in tables 4.1 and 4.2. First, the R^2 of the data-mining model developed by PolyAnalyst's Find Laws algorithm is shown. The R^2 for all of the rule-sets is very respectable, except for the urban district "Lang/Read" resultant model.

At one point it might be concluded that the language arts area does not lend itself to this analysis format, that the content is not tightly coupled enough, but that is proven untrue given the very high R^2 for suburban district 3, where the SAT verbal score was predicted from several of these same language arts independent variables.

The Pearson R correlation value is provided for each actual outcome vs. predicted outcome for the cohorts of 2001 and 2002. These values are also very respectable.

Finally, to determine how tightly the prediction rule-set was working, a paired-samples t-test was run on each matching set of data (actual vs. predicted dependent variable for 2001 and 2002 since these actual values were known). It was expected that the paired-samples t-test would yield no significant difference between the actual and predicted outcome scores. This was not always the case, as noted in tables 4.1 and 4.2. Upon review of the actual detailed data (student by student), I determined that the prediction model resulted in several outliers that, no doubt, are the reason for the significance in the paired-samples t-tests. The issue of why there are outliers and what other variables might be included in the prediction model rule-set are important follow-up questions.

The pilot study districts' data warehouses contain literally hundreds of variables that could have been included in the prediction rule-set. Which variables yield the best prediction model or which variables constitute key-leading indicators are critically important questions that need answers. This knowledge would help school leaders sort among the volumes of data to accurately design effective interventions and to discern whether those interventions are working.

Summary

This pilot study demonstrates that more affordable Artificial Intelligence tools can now be applied to the challenge of assisting school leaders in identifying key leading indicators on the outcome measures used to determine accountability under NCLB. Further, this work could lead to the development of more effective interventions for improving student achievement. The predictive modeling has been shown to work across four school districts from suburban to urban in Connecticut. Several follow-up questions emerge that are the subject of my continuing research:

1. For each year and content area of testing, as required by NCLB, what are the key leading indicators of success from year to year for proficiency in urban districts?
2. For each year and content area of testing, as required by NCLB, what are the key leading indicators of poor student achievement and what interventions are most successful at helping to improve achievement in urban districts?
3. When early childhood data are loaded into a data warehouse, what key leading indicators of poor performance (that represent "close-the-gap" cohorts) emerge and what interventions are most successful at thwarting poor performance by third grade in urban districts?
4. Will the use of additional independent variables (beyond those used in this pilot study) result in even more powerful rule-sets and prediction models in urban districts? Can more powerful prediction models reduce the outliers described in the pilot study? If so, what are those variables?
5. What level of granularity in the independent variables (total score, subtest score, object level score, item analysis level score) result in the most powerful prediction model rule-sets with the best cost-benefit ratio (powerful model vs. cost of collecting and analyzing more granular data)?

6. Can a general prediction model that covers the span of education impacted by NCLB be developed nationally across urban districts?
7. Regardless of school district type and size, are there common key-leading indicators that are universally important for the span of education covered by NCLB?
8. What interventions can be planned that utilize the results of these analyses, and what follow-up questions do school leaders have when presented these results in urban districts? What actions do school leaders take?
9. Once program participation is systematically coded and loaded into the data warehouse, can rule-sets be developed that show the effectiveness of those interventions in urban districts?

IMPLICATIONS AND WHAT THE FUTURE MAY HOLD

There are at least two important implications of the work discussed in this chapter for school leaders. First, it should be apparent that performing true root-cause analysis is challenging work requiring special skills and tools. There does not appear to be a quick and easy way to complete this analysis, and the currently available data warehousing query tools are not designed for this level of analysis. While it may be possible to eyeball statistics when using the data warehouse (and I will admit to having done that now and then myself), really *knowing* which variables matter most—the key leading indicators—takes hard work, special skills, and very special software.

Second, the accountability demands on schools will only become more intense, driving the need to find what works and what does not so that we can focus our limited financial and human resources. While it should be apparent that there are some answers on the horizon to identifying the root cause of student achievement within the available data collected by schools, the reality is that we are not there yet. Artificial Intelligence software *is* being used in the private sector for this purpose, so one can understand why many business leaders expect educators to be able to do this work. Toward this end, popular processes, such as Six Sigma[9], which are highly specialized, statistically driven processes that seek to improve organizational functioning, are being applied to education. Yet it is doubtful that the measures educators collect, test scores and the like, are robust, numerous, or accurate enough to provide highly reliable results when used in these processes.

This discussion begs the question of whether we can get closer to the truth about which performance measures count (are most useful in designing interventions) and what programs work through root-cause analysis using some of these new Artificial Intelligence tools and techniques. Over the coming years I believe that Artificial Intelligence systems will assist us in identifying the root causes of student achievement (positive and poor) so as to better identify where we should focus interventions. If there are answers to these questions among school performance data, then Artificial Intelligence looks like the most promising way of unlocking these hidden truths.

Thus, while the future is promising, we have not reached our goal yet. There are important lessons here for school boards, state departments of education, and even the federal government—all of whom, from time to time, make pronouncements and enact laws asking educators to do work they are unequipped to perform. These issues will be the topic of chapter 6. Before we move on, however, let's look at what actual data-driven decision making looks like at each stage of the framework I have discussed. Chapter 5 presents a series of case studies to explain the nature of this work.

NOTES

1. P. A. Streifer, "Applying artificial intelligence to develop a system to provide useful data for the improvement of student performance as required by NCLB." (Paper presented at the meeting of the National Center for Educational Statistics Summer Data Conference, Washington, D.C., July 2003.)

2. Megaputer's PolyAnalyst, 120 West 7th St., Suite 310, Bloomington, IN 47404; 812-330-0110; www.megaputer.com.

3. V. Dhar and R. Stein, *Seven Methods for Transforming Corporate Data into Business Intelligence* (Upper Saddle River, N.J.: Prentice-Hall, 1997), 104–105.

4. Megaputer, *PolyAnalyst 4.5*, www.megaputer.com (accessed August 8, 2003).

5. K. N. Berk and P. Carey, *Data Analysis with Microsoft Excel* (Pacific Grove, Calif.: Duxbury, 2000).

6. S. Carroll and D. Carroll, *Statistics Made Simple for School Leaders: Data-Driven Decision Making* (Lanham, Md.: Scarecrow Education, 2002).

7. T. Creighton, *Schools and Data: The Educator's Guide for Using Data to Improve Decision Making* (Thousand Oaks, Calif.: Corwin Press, 2000).

8. J. Utts, *Seeing through Statistics*, 2d ed. (Florence, Ky.: Brooks Cole, 1999).

9. P. Pande, R. Neuman, and R. Cavanaugh, *The Six Sigma Way Team Fieldbook: An Implementation Guide for Process Improvement Teams*, 1st ed. (Hightstown, N.J.: McGraw-Hill Trade, 2000).

Chapter Five

Case Studies/Examples

What does a typical data-driven decision-making process look like? Throughout this book I have been referring to the hard work that data-driven decision making requires. So far I have presented a range of examples from those that are fairly straightforward, such as those discussed in chapter 3, to the more complex examples of root-cause analysis and rule-based decision making in chapter 4. In this chapter I want to showcase several examples taken from my work with students and several districts over the past few years. These examples are a representative case-set of what the typical data-driven decision-making project encompasses and what one can expect in terms of actionable findings.

Interestingly, almost all of these examples were done without the assistance/use of a data warehouse, although access to one would have greatly facilitated progress. After the essential question was identified, the required data were obtained "the old-fashioned way"—some by hand, entering the data into Microsoft Excel, and others by extracting the data from the school's student information system and importing it into Excel.

Most analyses were performed with the statistical functions within Excel itself, Berk and Carey's *Data Analysis with Microsoft Excel*,[1] or the Statistical Package for the Social Sciences[2] (SPSS). The data that had to be collected by hand took months in some cases, and that time could have been shortened to hours with a data warehouse. Once the data were gathered, the process of organizing the data for proper analysis was undertaken. In many instances, we had to deal with missing or incomplete data, complicating the analysis. In the end, we worked for a useful outcome, but not an overextension of what the data were telling us about the problem under study. Thus, the following examples will demonstrate "what it takes to get this work done" and what is knowable in terms of actionable results.

In my University of Connecticut Executive Leadership Program, we include a full course on data-driven decision making. This is unique among leadership programs, but my students continue to tell me that they learn a great deal about how to do the work of data-driven decision making and what its limitations and real uses are. Thus, it remains an integral part of our university preparation for the superintendency. (As noted in my previous book, *Using Data for Making Better Educational Decisions*,[3] I was formerly superintendent of schools in Avon, Connecticut, and Barrington, Rhode Island, where I tested many of the ideas that eventually led to my work at the University of Connecticut.)

PRINCIPLES OF DDDM

Most of the examples used in this chapter are ones my students worked on during that course. They were required to select a problem that presents itself in their work setting, and then work through that problem using the principles of data-driven decision making. These principles include:

1. To what extent have you accounted for a systems model of school improvement—that changes in one area can affect another in unpredictable ways? What feedback system is in place to deal with these issues?
2. Have you clearly and concisely stated the problem in the form of a concept map?
3. Have you "chunked" the problem into "doable" analyses?
4. What stage of analysis is the question? Do you have access to the data in the format needed? Do you have the decision-support tools needed?
5. What has the data audit revealed? Are data readily accessible for the analysis?
6. What data do you need to create/collect?

7. Are the data in the form of aggregate group scores or individual student scores?
8. What are the metrics of the data? Are they scale scores, raw scores, nominal scores (i.e., yes/no), percentiles? Are they student performance portfolios? Writing samples, etc.? Are the data comparable? If not, what transformations are needed?
9. What statistical procedures are needed to address the problem?
10. What do you expect to learn from the analysis? What actions do you expect to take as a result of this work? What are your options for analysis and exploration? What information can you find to help?
11. Who else might have the same question(s)? Can you collaborate to share understandings/findings?
12. How can state standards and frameworks guide this inquiry?

I have found that it is virtually impossible to teach people how to do data-driven decision making unless they are working on real problems that are meaningful to them in their workplace. This is not surprising and is consistent with what we know about adult learning. Thus, my purpose in this chapter is not "to teach" data-driven decision making, but to demonstrate through various examples the range of questions that educators ask and what it takes to get that work done. Finally, there are a few examples included here that I have worked on as a consultant to districts—larger, more comprehensive studies. I have selected those that will be most meaningful to the purpose of this text.

In chapter 3 I presented a framework for thinking about your questions/problems. That framework, summarized, is as follows:

- Stage I: How did our school do compared to others?
- Stage II: What specific areas (and which students) contributed to our better performance?
- Stage III: Why did we do better? Can we predict?

To help demonstrate the application of this structure, the examples will be presented in this framework.

STAGE I: HOW DID OUR SCHOOL DO COMPARED TO OTHERS?

To answer this question, go to your state education website and a host of information will be accessible comparing your school's performance against others in your district and state. Here you can typically compare schools and districts on achievement measures, but in some cases more complex comparisons can be made across financial and human resource measures, among others.

Examples: Pennsylvania and Michigan

If you have access to the Internet please go to the website for Standard & Poor's School Evaluation Services, available at www.ses.standardandpoors.com.

Once you choose a state, you will be presented with a wide range of choices regarding what district or districts you want to view data from or what comparisons you want to see; you can also view Standard & Poor's "Observations" about a district's performance across a wide range of predetermined data points. There is also a "Quick Compare" function that allows you to compare four school districts' data against one another very easily.

By far, the Standard & Poor's website is the most comprehensive presentation of Stage I data used in the country. Currently, only two states have contracted with S&P to present these data—Michigan and Pennsylvania—although the system has been recently named a promising practice by the U.S. Department of Education and is slated for a national rollout.

The value of this system is that it provides easy access to a wide range of data for making comparisons across school districts. You can quickly determine how your district is performing compared to either those that S&P has chosen for your comparison group (based on a range of comparative variables) or those that you select. And because S&P has included far more than just student achievement data, this website provides the broadest possible external window into the operation of the schools.

The problem associated with Stage I data is that you cannot know the reasons for apparently good or poor performance. To address this issue with the S&P website, I had the opportunity to work with the Pennsylvania

Association of School Administrators to review the website. We developed the "Interpretive Guide & Technical Reference for the S&P School Evaluation Services," available at www.pasa-net.org/www/index.html.[4] The purpose of the Interpretive Guide is to provide superintendents an enhanced understanding of the comparisons made by S&P so that they can better interpret the data findings to their boards, communities, and staff.

Another example of Stage I data is Connecticut's CMT Reports website. CMT stands for the "Connecticut Mastery Test" currently administered in grades four, six, eight, and ten, but it is soon to include all intervening grades to comply with No Child Left Behind. Like Standard and Poor's website, but with much more limited data, the public can compare their schools/districts with others in the state. The website is www.cmtreports.com (use the interactive report function); you will need Internet Explorer 5.5 or better to view the complete site.[5]

To see what your state places on the Internet, go to the U.S. Department of Education's website: bcol02.ed.gov/Programs/EROD/org_list_by_territory.cfm.[6]

From there, click on your state, and then navigate to "State Education Agency (State Department of Education)" listed under the section titled "State Services and Resources." Once at your state's education website, you will have to navigate to the section where comparative data are presented, as each one is different. Most state's now include a website where Stage I data are presented.

MOVING FROM STAGE I TO STAGE II

The Corning-Painted Post School District (Corning, New York) embarked on a comprehensive school reform effort and they wanted it data driven. The district brought in Anthony (Tony) Wagner[7] to provide the conceptual frame for the effort named "Quantum Leap." I was asked to perform a data audit for the district, essentially to determine whether the data were available to meet the goals of Quantum Leap and, if not, how to go about collecting and codifying those data in a way that would be most useful.

The Corning-Painted Post School District commissioned this study to determine what steps should be taken to promote the availability of data for use by district leaders, Board of Education members, and instructional personnel. The study focused on current data-related practices to identify areas for improvement in the gathering and application of educational data. To that end, the following questions shaped and guided the development of the "data map" for the district:

- What data does the district have or need to address its goals and objectives, both in terms of measuring success in reaching goals and in making better decisions about future activities? Thus, what data are collected? In what format is data collected, where is it stored, and how is it made available?
- What data is currently used and how is it used?
- What additional data needs to be collected? How do the district's data collection practices need to change in light of the requirements of the No Child Left Behind statute and regulations?
- What infrastructure is in place to support the collection and use of data?
- What additional systems might be used to make data more accessible to the various audiences (school board, district administrative personnel, teachers, parents, and media) that need access to selected data from time to time?
- What processes should the district implement to develop a culture that values and understands data as a vehicle for systemic improvement?

The district had access to a wide range of Stage I data available from the New York State Department of Education's website and various paper reports. It also had a great deal of detailed data on student achievement, but those data were housed all around the district in various formats and databases—a similar condition found in many districts across the country. Thus, the district, knowing that Stage I data were not detailed enough to drive instructional improvement and not knowing if they had the right data for their improvement initiative, conducted the data audit.

As I began my work in Corning-Painted Post, I observed a powerful example of how Stage I data can be used persuasively. At a convocation exercise of the entire district staff to kick off the initiative, their superintendent, Dr. Donald Trombley, wanted to demonstrate to the staff the impact of poor student achievement. To do this, he asked ten students to assist him that day. As he discussed various performance outcomes, such as percent attendance, graduation rate, mastery rate on state tests, and so on, he also asked the relevant number of students to sit down, demonstrating the impact on real lives. After several of these examples, Dr. Trombley turned his attention to the new New York State Regents requirements—that students pass all five regents tests to graduate from high school. At that point, he asked four of the ten students to sit down, demonstrating that, unless the district acted now, they projected only 60 percent of the current freshman class would graduate from high school. Don Trombley's presentation, which followed Tony Wagner's, was one of the most impressive uses of Stage I data that I have seen.

Over the next several months, I performed the data audit with the assistance of three colleagues: Dr. Richard Kisiel, superintendent of schools, Avon, Connecticut; Mr. Larry Schaefer, assistant superintendent in Milford, Connecticut; and Mr. Aleck Johnson, formerly with the American Association of School Administrators and now an independent consultant. The project turned out to be a massive study, far too much detail to include here. The purpose of the study was to advance the district from Stage I data, which frames where performance lies today in relationship to other schools and districts, to Stage II data, where one can learn what specific areas (and which students) contribute to performance and where interventions might be focused to make improvements.

The findings and recommendations of the data audit covered many topics and was fairly detailed, providing a framework for the district to move forward in achieving its goals. Here are just a few of the findings and recommendations with some additional comments relative to this text:

- Interviews revealed that the staff did not feel it needed any "new" data, that they already had all the data points needed for making the kind of improvements they know are necessary. The key issue that emerged was how to provide access to the data in a timely way to those who need it.
- We learned that the district already collects a wide range of data, from student demographics to various forms of local, state, and national assessments, to program participation, staffing, and financial data. Thus, like so many districts with which I have worked, the problem shifts from data collection to data access. The problem facing Corning-Painted Post is that these data are in various formats and held in disparate databases. As a result, a major recommendation was to acquire a data warehousing system.

- We have learned from the practice of data-driven decision making that establishing a positive culture within the educational community for using data is critical to long-term success. Therefore, one of the questions driving the study asked, "What processes should the district implement to develop a culture that values and understands data as a vehicle for systemic improvement?" Our findings on culture were positive yet focused on the issue of establishing enabling policies. We found that staff was generally ready to move forward with the data-driven environment, but they need to comprehend fully the limitations and uses of standardized tests. Many also seek a better understanding of how to judge student progress when reviewing a wealth of data about a student or groups of students. Teachers also need access to data without placing heavy time demands on them to master and then pursue data analysis and reporting. Finally, many teachers and other staff were concerned that policies regarding fair and proper use of data be effectively implemented as part of any DDDM initiative. Again, these are common needs in many districts, so Corning-Painted Post is not alone here.
- We identified four levels of data users in the district. At one level, teachers want to use both current and longitudinal data about their students. Thus, for teachers an ideal decision-support system would be one in which they could input classroom and other assessment data *via* the Internet or other in-house system and then have access to those data in conjunction with all the other relevant data on their students. (In Connecticut there are several districts that are building their own version of such a system—one of which is Farmington, Connecticut.) At the next level, building administrators and department heads will want access to aggregations of selected data to spot trends across their units of responsibility. At the third level, senior administrators and the school board members will want to see these levels of aggregation across all departments and schools. Finally, from all of the data selected, reports on progress can be made available to the public via the Internet.
- If the district moves to a data warehousing system, there are important security considerations. The district will need to address the security issues that arise when student and other district data are made available through a data warehouse.

There are two issues here: policy and technology. The policy issue has to do with who has access and what they do with the data. All of these data are protected under the Family Educational Rights and Privacy Act (FERPA), the federal law that governs confidentiality of student data records. Whether data are in a paper or electronic file, they are still student records and need to be protected. Thus, whatever policies and procedures the district already has in place to protect all of these data in their current format will not change when data are provided to staff in other ways. (Several years ago, we thought that access to student data would become a volatile issue in school districts. This has not been the case, due, in part, to the care that districts have taken with respect to the release of data.)

A safe rule to follow is to provide access only to those individuals responsible for student information and to have policies in place governing how those data should be used (e.g., not releasing specific information on one child to the parent of another child; keeping public reports at the aggregation level to protect individual student data from release). By following basic rules and policies, many districts throughout the country have successfully navigated these thorny issues while providing teachers and staff access to the data they need.

The second security issue has to do with the technology. No electronic data storage system is completely hacker proof—even the federal government from time to time has its systems hacked (broken into). Any good data warehouse/information system will be protected by various firewalls and/or Internet security procedures/technology. Without additional cost, these systems provide the same level of security as online banking systems. While not perfect, they are very good.

- In addition to providing professional development to teachers and administration on the use and interpretation of various data, as required in all districts, written policies regarding the fair use of data should be developed at the administrative and board levels. A policy should be developed concerning teacher evaluation, specifying that student-testing data should not be used as prima facie evidence of teacher effectiveness. There are just too many threats to the validity and reliability of these data to make them suitable for use in this context. This policy should state that student-testing data should be reviewed and used by staff in their planning (once these data are more easily accessible and in the formats needed) and can be used in the supervisory process. This should be an important part of a data fair-use policy for staff supervision and evaluation. Once again, these are not unique issues for Corning-Painted Post, but ones I find in all the districts with which I work.

The Corning-Painted Post study is important because it focuses on the use of data to guide a well-thought-out school improvement effort. In the context of this book, the Corning-Painted Post work represents what many districts experience once they decide to move from Stage I data to Stage II data, which requires data that are more detailed for review and analysis.

STAGE II EXAMPLES OF DATA-DRIVEN DECISION MAKING

In this section I will describe several of my students' projects as they tackled real issues in their schools that required a data-driven approach. As I noted earlier, none of these examples were performed using a data warehouse, but having one would have greatly expedited the work. More important, as one proceeds through these projects, there often are many follow-up questions, some thornier than the initial question itself. When data access is such a problem, you are unlikely to pursue those follow-up questions. This was a persistent challenge throughout the examples that follow, but to the extent time allowed throughout the semester, we managed to pursue some of these follow-up questions.

All of my students have remarked on how a data warehouse and decision-support system would have facilitated their efforts and would have helped them make better decisions overall as they would have spent more of their available time exploring these follow-up questions rather than allocating so much time to data access.

Stage II: Taking on a Tough Issue: How Reliable Are Class Grades?

One of the most interesting issues that I have worked on recently was in Simsbury, Connecticut. The district and community were concerned over whether the high school's grading system and culture was negatively impacting students' chances of gaining acceptance to their first-choice colleges and universities. In many cases, this included top-tier schools, but not always. Simsbury is one of the top-performing school districts in the nation, whose students consistently perform at the highest levels on state mastery tests and SATs. I became involved in the project when one of my students, Colleen Palmer (high school principal), and her superintendent, Dr. Joseph Townsley (a good friend), asked if I would assist in reviewing several analyses that had been conducted by various ad hoc committees to try to determine the efficacy and scope of the problem.

My review of the data and those analyses confirmed that there was a plausible relationship between the grading practices at Simsbury High School and acceptance rates at elite colleges and universities. Following my work, the district conducted several additional reviews and policy discussions resulting in a collaborative process to change the culture of class grading at the high school.

Now this might sound rather simple and overstated—that teachers need to give higher grades—but it is not that simple. Teachers rightfully felt that their students had performed extremely well in the past and asked why a somewhat artificial change in standards was necessary. I spoke with the Director of Guidance about the changing nature of higher education, that competitive colleges must find some way to winnow down the number of applicants they receive, and one way they do this is through the grade point average (GPA). Thus, we argued, regardless of how justified the staff were, Simsbury students are likely put at a disadvantage if the school's grading practices are not in alignment with their peers both in the state and across the country.

A novel interim solution was presented by a local resident, Robert Hartranft (a retired nuclear engineer and former Naval officer), to present a balanced picture of student achievement to prospective colleges. His proposal was to chart the relationship between the local GPA for a given student and a national comparison of similar grades vs. SAT scores. The chart would take into account the relationship between Simsbury's grading standards and the national scene. At first, this idea seemed not viable, and many folks labored to develop something that made sense. In the end, Colleen Palmer and Bob Hartranft developed a chart for each student that displays this information—an example of which is presented in figure 5.1.

In this example, the student's (Mary Middle's) Simsbury High School (SHS) GPA of "16"—actually just shy of 16—is plotted against the school's SAT I Total score trendline to indicate that student's equivalent

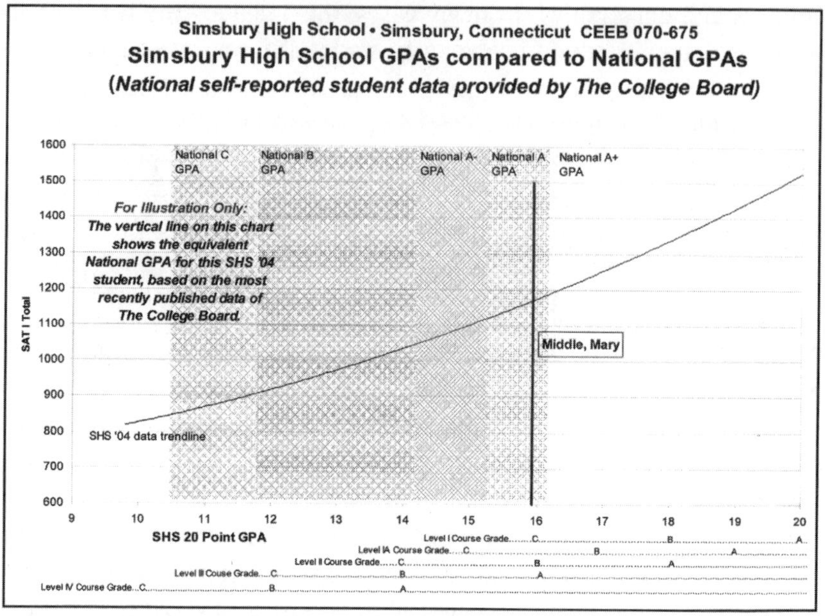

Figure 5.1. Simsbury High School GPAs compared to national GPAs

National GPA (in this case an "A"). Also presented is the student's GPA set against the SHS 20-point GPA scale and compared with the school's leveled courses/grades. Thus, on one chart we can see how Mary Middle's GPA compares with the national self-reported student GPA as reported by College Board (the most reliable information available). As students apply to colleges, the school sends out that student's chart along with the official transcript.

I thought this was an intriguing idea because I knew that imposing an "easier" grading standard would not work; staff needed time to explore their grading practices against curriculum standards and comparative practices in other schools. Yet, I also felt that students were truly disadvantaged by Simsbury's grading standards; Bob's initial idea, if developed fully, could provide an interim solution for the school.

I asked Bob where he got the idea to do this and he replied, "It was an earlier version of this table which provided the 'aha!' moment for me in July 2000: as soon as I saw it, I realized that I could translate SHS grades and deciles to national equivalents if the College Board would give me the underlying plots. They did, and I did." Cool! The basic reference document that Bob used was one of the College Board's Research Notes on High School Grading Practices.[8]

I have been impressed with the professionalism with which the district staff tackled this tough data-driven issue. By working together—community members, teachers, administrators, and the Board—the issue will be resolved over time. In fact the latest results I have seen from the school indicate that they are already well on their way. This example is unsurpassed, where a staff, administration, board, and community came together to successfully address one of the toughest issues in education—high school grading standards—using the principles of data-driven decision making to identify the problem and help design improvement strategies. A status report of the district's progress on this issue has been posted on the Internet at www.simsbury.k12.ct.us/shs/shswhitepaper060403r.pdf.

Stage II: The Achievement Gap

Colleen had just accepted the position of Simsbury High School principal but was not to begin her duties there until summer 2002. During that spring, she served as principal of another large, comprehensive high school, and she wanted to work on a project that would (1) prep her for her upcoming challenge in Simsbury and (2) address a problem at her current school. Thus, as part of her work with me, Colleen performed a mini-study to broaden her understanding of the following problem statement: "Determine if the differences in levels of achievement, as measured by GPAs (weighted and nonweighted), class rank, and SAT's, is statistically significant between subgroups of students stratified by gender and ethnic/racial classifications."

This problem is an important one, common among school leaders attempting to understand the achievement gap and the necessary interventions for improvements. But the process of constructing a meaningful set of questions, and then properly conducting the necessary analyses, is hard work. The problem statement was broken down into researchable analyses—a necessary step in deconstructing the bigger question into a set of steps that can be analyzed as follows:

- To what extent is there a current achievement gap between subgroups based on gender and ethnic/racial classifications?

- If a gap exists, does it exist in similar patterns for all stated indicators of achievement?

Then we decided to break this down even further by asking the following questions:

- How does GPA compare with SAT scores: (1) overall, (2) math course(s) GPA with math SAT, and (3) English GPA with verbal SAT?
- What effect do the (course) level designations for freshman year have upon the four-year sequence of classes and subsequent achievement of students?

As you might imagine the first set of questions was tough to analyze, while the second set was even more difficult. The first set directly addresses whether there is a problem, and the second set attempts to uncover deeper understandings about what might be going on that contributes to poorer (or better) performance later on in high school. These are all great questions, worthy of the required time and effort to find the answers.

All the data needed for the study resided in the school's student information system except SAT scores. Thus, after the required data were exported from the student information system into a spreadsheet, the SAT scores were entered by hand from hard copies available from the guidance department. While this took a lot of secretarial time, it was critically important to get all of these data into one place for proper analysis. To ensure that she had accurate data, Colleen carefully scrutinized the data for twenty-five randomly selected students to check for accuracy.

I worked with Colleen on the actual statistics to address these questions—as these became quite complex, beyond the scope of this book. But it makes the point that when a top-notch school leader wants to address an important issue, such as achievement gap analysis, it often entails sophisticated analyses to address their questions.

I recognize that statistics is sometimes a frightful subject, but I am always amazed at how complex and important school leaders' questions are and what it really takes to answer those questions. In my classes, I ask students to pick a problem that is important to them in their current work setting. Since Colleen was working in an urban school at the time, the achievement gap was a pressing issue. And she was moving to a high-performance district about to address a very tough grading policy issue that required a deep understanding of how GPA was related, or could be related, to standardized test scores. Thus, this problem was authentic for her. As she and I worked to parse the problem into doable analyses, we settled on the ones listed.

My view of data-driven decision making does not envision that every school leader will become a master statistician; this is simply impractical. But data-driven decision making does require at least an understanding of what the statistics can do and the degree to which the findings are useful in any way (issues of reliability, validity, and limitations of various statistical operations). Armed with this basic information, a statistician can be found/hired to do this more complex work. In Colleen's case, she understood these issues and even possessed a fair amount of statistical knowledge. I only helped with running the actual stats.

Achievement Gap Analysis Findings

To determine the differences by ethnicity/race in GPAs, class rank, and SATs, we used Analysis of Variance. Similar analyses were used for gender breakdowns on these variables. Colleen found that there was a statistical difference between the scores of the four subgroups of ethnic/racial designations in all areas of achievement. Thus, we had an answer to the first and second questions—for this cohort of students there is an achievement gap across all variables studied. We did not find as clear evidence for the gender issue, especially in the math content area, where there was not a statistical difference between boys and girls. However, girls outscored boys regardless. From a statistical point of view, this would require deeper analysis to understand what is occurring. Thus, I would refer back to my 3x3 matrix in which actionable steps should only be taken after analyses like these are performed on at least three cohorts.

To address the second set of questions that seek to compare student achievement in selected course content to their comparison standardized testing content, more complicated analyses were needed. For example, an analysis of covariance was run with the composite SAT score as the covariate, the department grade as the dependent variable, and the department code as the independent variable. The result indicated that even while adjusting grades based upon SAT scores (that's what analysis of covariance can do), there remained significant differences in grades (by department) beyond the differences in SAT scores. There were several other analyses run, but, as Colleen said in her final paper on this issue,

> while these findings were certainly interesting, they led to the asking of other questions related to student achievement and the interrelationships with other factors in school to understand more completely the complexity of learning and "spheres of influence" that affect student learning.

As always happens doing this work, initial questions and their analyses yield answers that only beget further questions. Broad understanding of the achievement gap issue in this school would require, at the least, running these same analyses over additional cohorts, but Colleen was hampered in her work by not having these data in a data warehouse because a great deal of her time was spent on preparing the data for analysis. As she reflected on all of this, she wrote the following summary:

> During this preliminary exploration of data, the achievement gap between ethnic/racial subgroups was confirmed and quantified. While it was common knowledge that the gap existed, by quantifying the difference, the school now has data for the status of the achievement gap for the year 2001. This same exercise could be conducted for each of the past six years (SASI database has data for past six years) to track trends. Given the importance of the issue, at least 2 or 3 more years would be prudent. While tremendous strides have been made to increase educational opportunities for minority students over the past eight years, have these efforts made a difference, especially to the majority minority, African-Americans, or did it just make us administrators feel better that we tried so hard! Anecdotal data is no substitute for quantifiable data. Progress of students cannot be rated by the effort expended to improve learning; it can only be rated by measurable student outcomes. Were the interventions to reduce the achievement gap effective? Only the data combined with sound reasoning abilities can answer that question.
>
> Further questions to explore that were prompted by this exercise are:
>
> 1. What relationship to learning do course grades really have? What do grades really mean? Are grades linked to measurable student outcomes

standardized within a school? If yes, what does that tell us, if not, what use are grades?

2. Why did the girls outperform the boys on the SAT mathematics? I would like to see a histogram of the patterns of distribution of grades—what might this tell me? What were the enrollments (by gender) in each level of study for junior math classes? The CAPT (Connecticut Academic Performance Test) results for this class had boys outperforming girls—what changed between these two tests? It would again be worthwhile to examine the patterns of distribution. Did the band system of calculating CAPT goal distort the outcome? [Note by author: the bands that Colleen refers to are the same grouping designations now mandated by No Child Left Behind where a student's achievement score is placed into 1, 2, or 3 performance designations—basically goal, proficient, or needs improvement.]
3. What implications for teaching and learning might result by a discussion of the average GPA in each department with the departmental directors? How can data prompt decision-making? How does data contribute to informed intuition? Data that are organized in meaningful ways provide us with information with which we are more likely to make decisions that will enhance learning opportunities for students.
4. As I contemplate my role as principal, it is critical to understand to what extent that data may be used for analysis if no data warehouse is available. I was pleasantly surprised that even with this limited spreadsheet I was able to extract useful information. Given that I most likely will not have access to a data warehouse for next year, I would like to explore how far I can go in my analysis with a reasonable amount of human resource energy to develop these comprehensive spreadsheets.
5. Tracking continues to persist in high schools. Even though students are permitted to take more rigorous classes each year, while policy allows this shift, the school culture does not. I would be interested in tracing patterns of students who move from one level of study to another over four years, including those who move to a less rigorous level as well as those who opt for a more rigorous level.

If I were to remain in my current position, I would complete a similar analysis for all six years of data that are available. It would be valuable to determine the greatest predictor of minority student achievement at the high school level. Or what course-taking pattern most represented their achievement levels. Part of this inquiry would look at previous grades,

> CMT (Connecticut Mastery Test) scores, placement in level of study for the freshman year and other pertinent information. With all the research in the literature about the negative effects of tracking, it is my hypothesis that the phenomenon of tracking minority students into the lower levels of rigor of study during freshman year closes doors for access to more rigorous levels during subsequent years of study.

Conclusion

> While I have been afforded scores of hours of training in total quality management, my approach to continuous improvement has been hindered without the appropriate schools for systematic data collection and analysis. With the advent of the new technology for data warehousing, each administrator must become competent in the skills of planning for, improving and controlling the quality of the institution's processes and outcomes. This is an exciting time to prepare for the superintendency.

Colleen's work is an example of exceptional practice in data-guided decision making. She asked great questions, followed through on the analysis to the extent time and resources were available, interpreted those findings properly and, like so many of us who do this work, ended up only asking more questions. In my earlier book, I wrote that at some point in our research we need to stop the analysis process and move to a decision because of potential analysis/paralysis and cost-benefit considerations of what it really takes to complete this work. In the case of achievement gap inquiries, Colleen left her successor a sound foundation from which further analysis and actions could be planned. In the case of the Simsbury grading issue, the school's success in addressing the matter is in very large part attributable to the manner in which Colleen, Dr. Joseph Townsley (superintendent), and her staff approached the problem employing all the principles and techniques of data-driven decision making.

Stage II: To What Extent Do Specially Designed Programs at the Elementary Level Work to Improve Achievement?

Earlier in this book, I asked whether we could know if specially designed elementary programs had any real impact on student achievement in later grades. Short of doing the type of root-cause analysis I discussed in chapter 4, the issue is: "To what extent can we determine whether these programs are worth the time and expense using more typical analyses?" To demonstrate the possibilities, I have selected two examples of work performed by my students. The first explores the extent to which a specially designed reading program influences achievement, and the second addresses whether a multiage organizational schema meets its goals in relation to more traditional settings.

Does the Early Success Program Work?

Glen Peterson was principal of an elementary school in central Connecticut in 1998 when the district adopted the Houghton Mifflin Early Success program as the remedial reading program for grades one and two. Prior to this, the school used two other programs for kindergarten and grade one, but they had no remedial program for the higher grades. At the time Glen performed this mini-study, the school had been using the Early Success program for three years, and Glen questioned its effectiveness and cost benefit. The program was taught by a certified teacher who worked with small groups of students in each of the classrooms for about forty-five minutes per day. The district was experiencing financial pressures at the time; thus, Glen wanted to know if this program was worth retaining. Fortunately, there were adequate data to do this analysis, although it was all on paper and needed to be entered into an electronic spreadsheet for analysis.

Glen developed the following questions:

- While overall student academic achievement and reading proficiency are improving over time as measured by on- and off-level Connecticut Mastery Tests, which are given in grades three, four, and five, to what degree is the reading achievement of students receiving the Early Success program improving?
- Students selected to receive Early Success in grade two are in the lowest third of readers in their class. Over time, do they catch up to the grade level as a whole and to those students who are reading at grade level?
- To what degree is the Early Success program or the remedial programs in the primary grades responsible for the improvements in student reading achievement?

The first two questions are sufficiently complex to analyze, while the third is a question of root cause. Glen acknowledged the difficulty in addressing the third question when he wrote,

> This may be a very difficult question to answer because Early Success is only one of the many initiatives designed to raise academic and reading achievement that have been initiated during the last three years. We have also added summer school, after-school tutoring, homework club, paraprofessional support in the intermediate grades, CMT coaching, and we have substantially improved the elementary reading curriculum by changing from a whole class model to one that focuses on guided reading instruction in small groups.

As a result, Glen and I decided not to attempt this question; rather, we determined to intuit the overall value that the program might contribute to student achievement as a result of doing the first two analyses. In addition, we resolved to further focus those questions, which resulted in the following:

- To what extent does the Early Success program help the weakest second grade readers become proficient readers?
- Do the students receiving Early Success catch up to their peers?

Once we had focused our questions, Glen began determining what data were needed and which data were actually available, and started entering them into a spreadsheet with a structure that allowed for the required analysis. Glen's study is an important one because it reflects the typical questions that principals ask about program effectiveness, requiring a good deal of analysis to answer. Yet Glen did not have a data warehouse nor was he a statistician by trade. As you will see in the following pages, Glen uncovered some surprising findings after he scrutinized the data. In his own words, here is what he did and what he found.

> I decided to develop a database for students in the classes of 2007–2010, which includes the sixth graders who most recently left the school, and the current students in grades three through five. Students in the class of 2009, the current fourth grade students are the first ones to benefit from having the Early Success program available when they were in second grade. Fields in the database include: name, class, gender, lunch status, special education, primary language, summer school, retention, Early Success grade 1, Early

Success grade 2, as well as all CMT reading and writing test scores in grades three through five, and end of year reading tests.

DRP scores for the past two years have been entered into an Excel spreadsheet, but other information was only available on state CMT summary reports, or in students' individual files. Developing the database was time consuming, but it certainly took less than 40 hours to collect and input the data for 273 students in the four cohorts. A task of this size could easily be assigned to an administrative assistant, elementary school secretary, or talented paraprofessional. Although it has been recommended by data warehousing experts not to retroactively try and create databases, the task is a very valuable one that can be done in house at a small or medium sized elementary school over a reasonably short period of time.

Data Screening

One of the most time-consuming tasks related to the database was screening and cleaning the data. This process included both selecting and deselecting students to include in the database and converting Degrees of Reading Power (DRP) scores so they could be properly compared over time.

Our district has a highly mobile population. Of the 273 original students in the four classes, only 198 of them took the DRP in grades two, three, and four (or the DRP in both grades two and three for the current third graders). Students who hadn't taken the DRP for three consecutive years or two in the case of third graders were removed from the database to be analyzed. Similarly, it was also decided to remove most students receiving special education services from the database. Prior to the 2000 test administration, the State of Connecticut Department of Education (SDE) allowed greater numbers of special education students to be exempted from the testing. Although the number of exemptions at the school has been historically low (well below 10 percent), it was decided to remove four students in the class of 2008 from the database so the class makeup would be similar to the two preceding classes.

Touchstone Applied Science Associates (TASA), the developers of the DRP, report scores based on comprehension levels (p scores)—the Independent, Instructional, and Frustration levels. The DRP scale is an absolute value equal interval scale, and as such, scores can be converted from one comprehension level to another for comparison purposes. Scores in grades two through four are reported at the p=.70 level while fifth and sixth grade scores are reported at the p=.75 level. Converting DRP scores

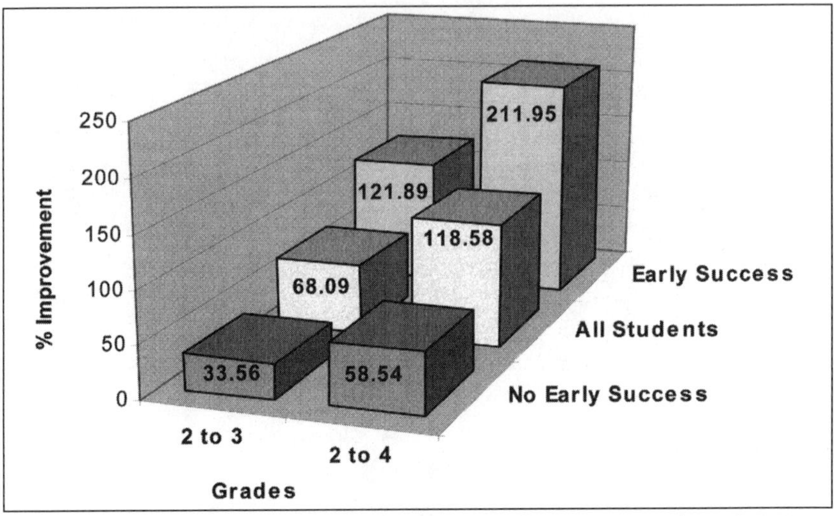

Figure 5.2. Grade to grade percentage improvement in DRP scores, class of 2009

from the p=.75 level of comprehension to the p=.70 level is simply a matter of adding 3 points to the p=.75 score. However, the DRP scale begins at 15 points. Many second grade non-readers fall below the 15 points and their scores are reported as 15-. These scores cannot be accurately compared to scores in subsequent years. Individual second grade scores are reported by TASA at both the p=.70 level and the p=.50 level. At p=.50, which is considered the frustration level, most second graders had a score of above 15. It was decided to convert all scores for all students to the p=.50 level throughout the database. However, second grade scores with a raw score below seven correct items still show a 15- score at the p=.50 level. TASA's DRP conversion charts do not provide conversion numbers for these scores so it was decided to give each of those students a score of 11 at the p=.50 level because it is the average of the possible scores between 7 and 15.

Data Analysis

The analysis of the DRP data included several measures: percentage change in DRP scores; percentage of students above goal and below remedial level; comparison of students who received Early Success to their class as a whole and to their peers who didn't receive the intervention; and finally, correlations and analysis of variance between Early Success participation and DRP scores.

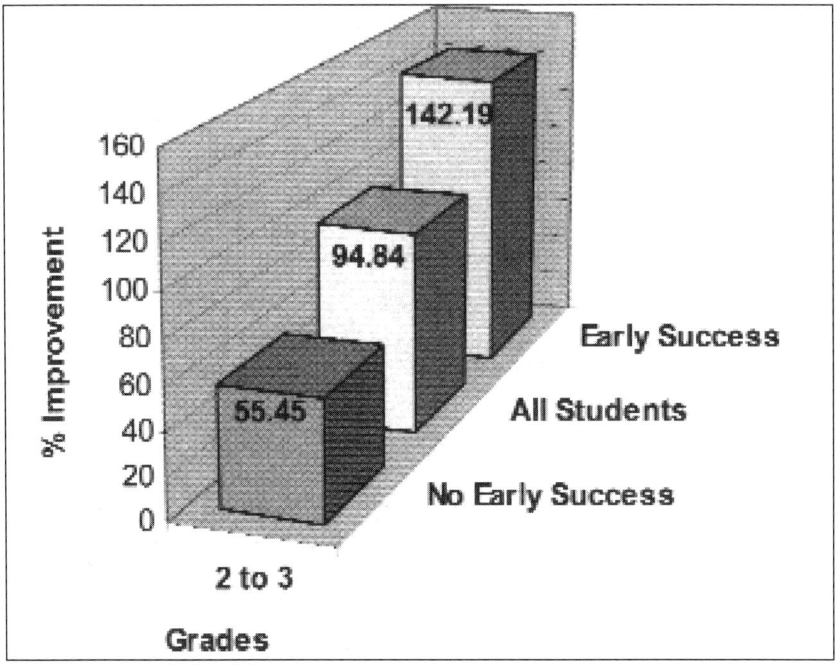

Figure 5.3. Second to third grade improvement in DRP scores, class of 2010

Figure 5.2 shows the overall improvement of DRP scores for students currently in fourth grade; this was the first class of students to have Early Success available when they were in grade two. The students as a whole, shown in yellow, improved by nearly 70 percent from grade two to grade three and had improved by nearly 120 percent by the time they reached grade four. For the students who had Early Success, the improvement was even more dramatic. Their scores improved by over 120 percent from grade two to grade three and by over 210 percent by the time they took the fourth grade mastery test. The students in the class of 2010 improved at an even higher rate from grade two to grade three as shown in figure 5.3.

Clearly the reading scores of students who have received the Early Success program in grade two have improved more than the scores of their peers on a percentage basis. This is to be expected as the Early Success students were among the poorest readers in grade two. The mean second grade DRP score for the group of students receiving Early Success in the class of 2009 was 19.26, well under the half of the mean score of their peers who didn't receive Early Success in grade two (45.11). We know that the Early Success students in the class of 2009 improved by 68 percent on the DRP

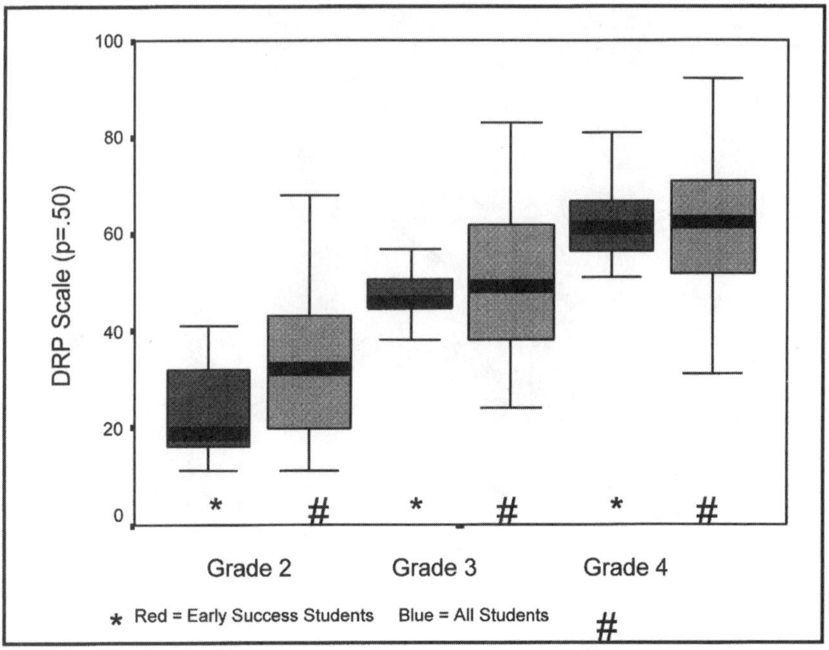

Figure 5.4. Mean DRP Scores of Early Success Students and All Students, Class of 2009 Gr. 2: ES = 57.05% of All; Gr. 3: ES = 78.36% of All; Gr. 4: ES = 86.42% of All

from grade two to three. The students who didn't receive Early Success would have had to improve by over 30 DRP points to achieve the same percentage increase.

Not only have the DRP scores of Early Success students risen dramatically from grades two to three to four, their scores are getting closer to those of all students in their grade.

In other words, the students receiving Early Success in grade two are catching up to their grade level as a whole and to their peers who were stronger second grade readers. Figures 5.4 and 5.5 show the degree to which the Early Success students are gaining ground in reading vis-à-vis their grade level as a whole. In both years the mean of the DRP test scores in grade two for Early Success students was less than 60 percent of the mean score for the entire grade cohort. By grade three, the mean of the Early Success students was above 74 percent of the mean or all students for both the 2009 and 2010 cohorts. The Early Success students in current fourth grader class of 2009 have reached 86 percent of the class as a whole.

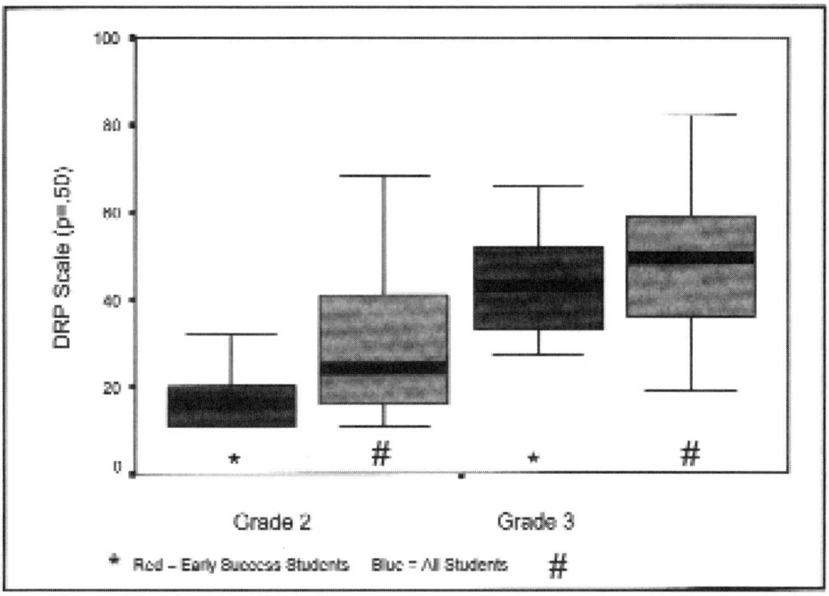

Figure 5.5. Mean DRP scores of Early Success Students and All Students, Class of 2010 Gr. 2: ES = 53.59% of All; Gr. 3: ES = 74.87% of All

The Early Success students as a whole are certainly catching up to their peers in terms of the DRP test. The achievement gap between the Early Success students and the entire grade level is shrinking. Furthermore, the numbers of Early Success students at DRP grade level goal is increasing and the number of Early Success students below the remedial level on the DRP is decreasing. Figure 5.6 shows the percentages of all students and Early Success students above goal and below the remedial level in the classes of 2009 and 2010.

From this evidence it is clear that the reading performance of the students receiving Early Success is improving rapidly. As a principal, I'm particularly proud that the percentage of Early Success students who fall below the remedial level on the DRP is rapidly shrinking over time. It is important to remember that students were selected for Early Success primarily because they fell below the remedial level on the grade two DRP. For the class of 2009 at least, the number of Early Success students below the remedial level fell by over 64 percent from grade two to grade four.

[Note: for this text, the sections on correlational analyses and Analyses of Variance have been omitted as they reflect levels of complexity that are beyond the scope of this book and unnecessary for interpreting this example.]

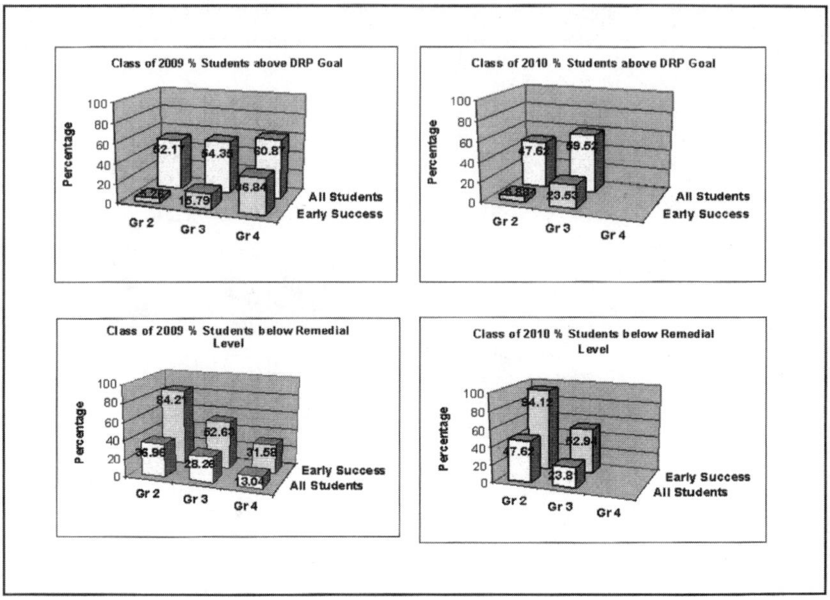

Figure 5.6. Percentage of students above DRP goal and below DRP remedial level in grades 2, 3, and 4 for the 2009 and 2010 classes

Drilling Down and Reframing the Questions

All of the data regarding the Early Success program and improvement in reading as measured by the DRP looked very positive. The only problem is that only one class of students (2009) has received Early Success in grade two and taken the DRP as part of fourth grade mastery testing. How could control groups be developed for previous classes of students to compare to the class of 2009?

Using the basic criteria for Early Success, students in the classes of 2007 and 2008, the current fifth and sixth graders, who scored below the remedial level on the DRP when they were in second grade, were selected as "Early Success-like" groups. The second grade reading profile and the number of students in these groups is similar to that of the Early Success groups in the classes of 2009 and 2010 who actually received the Early Success intervention.

Figure 5.7 shows that the improvement in DRP from grade two to three for the class of 2008, which didn't receive Early Success is only slightly lower than the improvement shown by the students in the class of 2009 and 2010 who actually received Early Success.

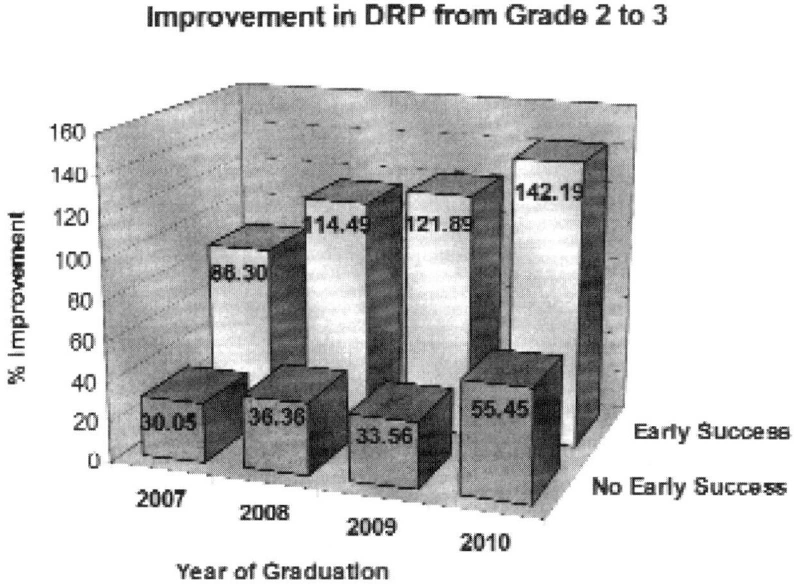

Figure 5.7. Improvement in DRP from Grade 2 to 3

From grade two to grade four, as shown in figure 5.8, the students who didn't receive the Early Success program in the class of 2008 actually made better gains than the students who had the benefit of the program the following year. Figure 5.8 shows that the DRP scores of the "Early Success-like" students in the class of 2008 improved by 224.30 percent while the same scores for actual Early Success students in the class of 2009 improved by 211.95 percent. Fifty percent of the "Early Success-like" students in the class of 2008 achieved goal on the fourth grade DRP while only 31.81 percent of the 2009 Early Success students reached this level. The numbers of the Early Success groups falling below the remedial level in grade four were very close.

What Does It All Mean?

I was very surprised to find the achievement of the control group students in the class of 2008 was better than that of the actual Early Success students in the class of 2009. The achievement level of the control group in the class of 2007 was well below that of the Early Success students of 2009 and 2010.

One must certainly ask the question that if students who didn't receive the remedial reading program in grade two actually performed better than students who received the program, is the program worth keeping?

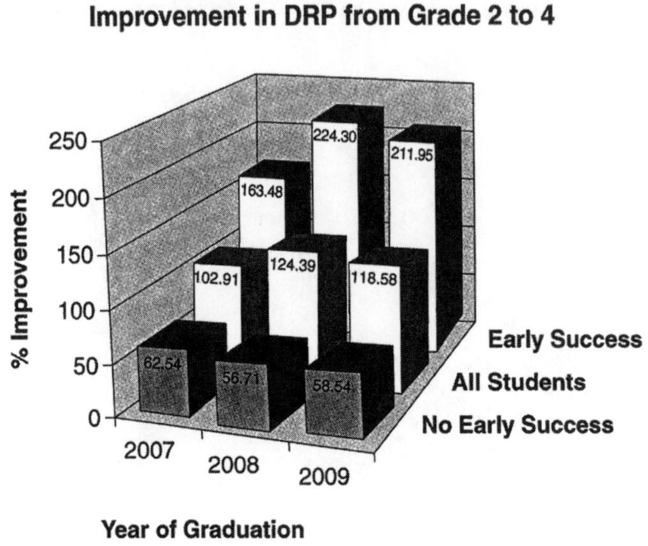

Figure 5.8. Improvement in DRP from Grade 2 to 4

One would certainly expect the scores of the students who received the remedial program to far surpass those of the control groups who didn't receive the intervention. Of course, other factors come into play. For one thing, the class of 2008 had the highest fourth grade DRP scores in the history of the school. The students chosen for the control groups, who seem similar to the Early Success students in grade two, may not be good matches. We may simply have too few cohorts of students to make any generalizations regarding the efficacy of the Early Success program. We may need another year or two of concrete data to answer these questions adequately.

This analysis certainly supports taking a closer look at the components of the Early Success program: staff, supervision, training, curriculum, and the lesson delivery model. It also makes sense to work to discuss the results of this analysis with the Early Success staff to work to improve the program, and look into other remedial reading programs.

As a final note, this study only looked into changes in the annual DRP scores. Other important measures of reading achievement such as classroom grades, running records, guided reading level, and Development Reading Assessments (DRA) were not taken into account because they fell beyond the scope of this analysis. Those other outcome variables would need to be considered before any final determination regarding the Early Success program could be made.

The Bigger Question

Now, after conducting these analyses, let's get back to the bigger picture and most important question: upon review of this analysis, would you keep the program in light of tough financial pressures on the school? After doing this work, Glen decided to keep the program because he felt he did not have enough persuasive evidence that the program *was not* working. He had only researched two cohorts and he recognized that there could be any number of other intervening variables contributing to overall achievement levels. As Glen rightly admitted, a number of variables, when taken all together, may contribute to the success of these students and prematurely shutting down this program could or could not be the right move.

This mini-study reminds me of the example I used in chapter 3 where, after doing the analysis on Reading Recovery, we wondered if the second- or third-grade teachers could be as responsible for long-term student success as the Reading Recovery program in grade one. The truth is that it was probably all of these factors and influences converging to contribute to student success. Data-driven decision making can help you determine, at least to some extent, whether the program or variable under study is in some way contributing to achievement, but it is very difficult to isolate a single program impact. In Glen's case, the Early Success program had only been in place one year; thus, it was too early to make a definitive judgment. Glen recognized the need for a 3×3 study of these variables, which could be quickly accomplished if all the required data were in a data warehouse or if he had more time to work by hand.

Since completing this study, Glen has become principal of the East Hartford–Glastonbury (Connecticut) Elementary Magnet School, and he is near completion of his doctoral studies at the University of Connecticut. The mini-study described here shows what can be done to address important questions even in environments that do not have a wealth of resources. Interestingly, we did not intend to do the control group analysis; this only emerged as an issue after analyzing the data for the initial questions. However, you can distinguish the impact on decision making with this additional analysis. Again, this is a typical circumstance in this work.

To summarize the process, the initial questions require new focus. Next, the data must be collected as they are not always in a place and format required for analysis. Third, cleaning the data for readiness takes time and effort unless there is a data warehouse in place. Even then, the data need to have been loaded into the data warehouse (which sometimes hasn't been done because some of these data are not considered important enough to load until an administrator asks a question about achievement). Fourth, the analysis work must be completed, which takes time and skill. Fifth, the initial data analysis typically results in answers that only beget other questions for follow-up study. And finally, completing this work, more often than not, results in findings that are less than definitive, that may only inform your intuition about what should be done.

Multiage Grade 1/2 and Traditional Classrooms: Is There a Difference in Student Performance?

Viktor Toth is principal of the Woodstock Elementary School in Woodstock, Connecticut. His school has had a grade one-two multiage configuration for some time and he wanted to know if students in that program perform as well as those in the other, more traditional classroom settings. His research questions were driving at whether the administration should continue the Multiage Program. But, for the purposes of this mini-study, we focused specifically on these questions:

- To what extent is there a difference in student preparation and performance between the two programs?
- To what extent do students taught in multiage classrooms perform better or worse than their peers in the traditional program?

Viktor then assembled the needed data that included Cognitive Abilities Test (CogAT) and Connecticut Mastery Test data for the two cohorts: Multiage students (students who remained in the same Multiage classroom for two years, as first and second graders) and Traditional students (students who attended separate first- and second-grade classrooms). He looked at three cohorts of students over a two-year period, thus achieving a 3×2 cohort analysis model as follows:

- The Fourth-Grade Class of 2000
  - 1999 Grade three CogAT

  —2000 Grade four CMT
- The Fourth-Grade Class of 2001
  —2000 Grade three CogAT
  —2001 Grade four CMT
- The Fourth-Grade Class of 2002
  —2001 Grade three CogAT
  —2002 Grade four CMT

The CogAT includes various assessments that measure the development of cognitive skills in the verbal, quantitative, and nonverbal areas. Thus, taken together with the content areas measured by the Connecticut Mastery Test, these two assessments formed the basis for Viktor's analysis. Fortunately, all of these data were available, although the CogATs were only in paper report format. That presented a serious challenge because Viktor needed to transform those paper reports into electronic format. Viktor is adept at computer skills and was able to use an electronic program to scan these pages, which then put the data into a readable spreadsheet format. Cool! Thus, once these data were scanned and exported into Excel, he parsed the data into a more usable columnar format.

Viktor did not have a data warehouse, so the Connecticut Mastery Test data also had to be extracted from its native electronic format (each Connecticut school and district receives data diskettes with their achievement data, but these files are not very useful in their native formats). To do this Viktor used a program provided by the Connecticut Department of Education that performs the extraction, although this program requires a rather steep learning curve to use effectively. But because Viktor has these skills, using the program was not a challenge for him.

At this point Viktor had data in two different data sets and formats—one in the CogAT extract and the other for the CMT extract. These needed to be combined into one Excel spreadsheet. To do this we performed our own version of data transformation and loading.

We brought all the disparate Excel spreadsheets into Microsoft Access, a database program, and we built a small database. The development of that database, how it is done, is beyond the scope of this text. But interestingly, many of my students generate questions that require the building of a database for analysis. Thus, the process Viktor followed here was repeated in a number of the projects I have worked on with students. If we had access to a data warehouse, most of this work would have been unnecessary.

Analysis and Findings

To determine if there were differences in achievement across the various measures under study, we used analysis of variances techniques. The analyses between groups (Multiage and Traditional) showed that the groups were balanced in terms of ability—at least as measured by the CogATs. This knowledge is important in order to allow for a proper interpretation of the follow-up analyses between groups on achievement. The achievement analysis also showed no statistical difference between the Multiage and Traditional groups. To be fair to the study, Viktor performed a number of analyses that are only summarized here, but my purpose is not a review of statistical technique. In fact, there are even more sophisticated statistical models that we could have employed but chose not to because our goal was to attempt analysis with the tools and techniques available to most mortals!

In his presentation, Viktor highlighted the following findings and recommendations. First, the two groups are well balanced in terms of students' abilities. Second, the statistical analyses demonstrated that there is no difference between the Multiage and Traditional groups in achievement. (I was also satisfied that there were no practical differences, either.) Thus, both programs are achieving the same results. And finally, since there is no additional cost to the Multiage program and because students are equally served, the Multiage program should be retained.

STAGE III—CAN WE PREDICT HIGH SCHOOL ACHIEVEMENT?

The previous examples discussed in this chapter have been either Stage I or Stage II analyses. In chapter 4, I discussed the application of Artificial Intelligence software to the challenge of doing root-cause analysis. I will close this chapter with the application of this technology by one of my students toward an issue his school was addressing.

Dr. David Harriger was principal of a small high school in Connecticut and wanted to determine the best predictors of high school GPA and PSAT from the earlier state mastery tests in grade six, eight, and ten. He argued that it would be beneficial to know if earlier student performance accurately predicted GPA and PSAT so that the district could concentrate curriculum alignment efforts in a targeted format through early intervention to help improve student success in high school and enhance college acceptance opportunities.

David collected a range of data from two classes of students, each going back to when these students were in sixth grade. Thus, this was a 2×6 model: two cohorts retracing five years each (twelfth GPA back to sixth-grade mastery test). He captured reading and math scores from the sixth- and eighth-grade state mastery tests. He also collected the reading, math, and science scores from the tenth-grade state mastery test called the Connecticut Academic Performance Test (CAPT). His data set included the PSAT verbal, math, and writing scores along with the students' eleventh- and twelfth-grade GPAs. David put all the data into Excel spreadsheets, retaining only students for whom all data were present.

We performed multiple regression analyses using Megaputer's PolyAnalyst (Artificial Intelligence) program that I discussed in chapter 4 to determine the extent to which student performance variables could predict a student's GPA in high school. The regression analyses were successful at identifying which scores were good predictors of GPA; additionally, the software yields a prediction rule-set (and associated statistics) that allows one to understand which variables are most important in the prediction model.

We learned that tenth-grade CAPT reading was the most reliable predictor for student GPA, followed by CAPT math, which is not too surprising given that CAPT and GPA are more closely proximate with one another as high school measures of achievement. Then, the prediction rule-set also indicated that certain subtests from sixth and eighth grade could be useful as shown in the following rule-set (see chapter 4 for a more thorough discussion on the interpretation and use of these rule-sets):

GPA = + 33.5781 + 0.0591113*captread + 0.0496153*captmath + 0.0273940*captsci + 0.0788219*cmt8math−0.0529345*cmt6read + 0.00925155*psatmath + 0.152121*psatw

Here we can see that essentially six variables emerged as important predictors of GPA and that these variables could be used by the software to apply to subsequent cohorts to predict GPA as discussed in chapter 4: PSAT writing; CAPT reading, math, and science; Connecticut Mastery Test (CMT) eighth-grade math; and CMT sixth-grade reading.

To explore this issue more deeply we used the "Find Laws" algorithm from Megaputer's PolyAnalyst program, conducting a number of analyses similar to those described in chapter 4. Here we wanted to know what variables could be best used to predict PSAT verbal scores. The software yielded the following rule-set:

PSAT_VERB 5 0.0962509 *captsci+0.240982 *cmt8read+0.0753744 *captread−14.672

The R^2 of this prediction model equaled 0.6999—a high value indicating that the prediction model is strong. Consequently, this rule-set could be applied to subsequent cohorts to predict their PSAT verbal scores using the eighth-grade CMT reading scores and their tenth-grade CAPT science and reading scores.

From all of the analyses we performed, David concluded that the best predictors for high school GPA are (in order of significance): CAPT reading, CAPT math, CMT eighth-grade math, and CMT eighth-grade reading. Finally, he recognized that more work would be needed, exploring these relationships over additional cohorts before drawing firm conclusions about curriculum modifications and alignment. But the important point is that we were able to demonstrate the application of these new technologies in a real-world school problem.

The pilot study I described in chapter 4 and this mini-study are the very beginnings of an entirely new world that Artificial Intelligence is opening up to assist educators in addressing very complex achievement challenges. David is a statistician—he understands how to apply regression analyses—however, he knew that the most he could ask from traditional regression models is to learn what the best predictors for a particular cohort *were*. To be sure, this information alone could be useful in addressing his essential question. But we wanted to take this issue one step further, to see if we could develop a prediction rule-set that could then be applied to subsequent cohorts—and we were successful. Unfortunately, the school does not have a data warehouse, so extracting the essential data for several additional cohorts was beyond the scope of David's work and he has now moved on to another position. When the district installs a data warehouse, further analyses would be possible with someone who possesses the same knowledge of statistics as David.

SUMMARY

From Stage I questions (such as comparing your school with another), to Stage II questions, (such as those explored by Colleen Palmer, Glen Peterson, and Viktor Toth), to Stage III questions (such as the issue of predicting GPA that David Harriger tackled), we can see that this is challenging and time-consuming work. But we can also see that real benefits are possible if one commits the time and resources to complete the work properly.

These are not unusual examples and they reflect the scope of a typical project in data-driven decision making. Almost all of these individuals had virtually no prior experience in performing this level of analysis before beginning their work; thus, this is something that almost everyone can do—albeit these are very talented educators.

You should also have noticed the fact that none of these "projects" benefited from having a data warehouse in place. As a result, these projects took much longer than they should have, with sometimes 80 percent or more of the time spent on data collection and formatting. If these educators had access to data warehouses, that 80 percent would have been reduced to 10 percent, leaving more time and energy for further analysis and exploration of the data.

The major theme of this book is to demonstrate what it takes to execute data-driven decision making. The examples in this chapter are among the models I offer in that regard. But they are not unique; there are many more being conducted every day by educators who are hard at work looking for ways to improve achievement.

Given the scope of the work needed to accomplish data-driven decision making, one must wonder whether the accountability demands of the twenty-first century are fair, given the resources and tools educators currently have at their disposal. The next chapter will explore the new accountability era and how it is influencing work in schools. If nothing else, the examples I present here should be a wake-up call for policy makers. It should show them just what is needed to carry out this work as they enact tighter controls on schools, requiring deeper and more sophisticated analyses of student performance.

NOTES

1. K. N. Berk and P. Carey, *Data Analysis with Microsoft Excel* (Pacific Grove, Pa.: Duxbury, 2000).

2. Statistical Package for the Social Sciences, *SPSS Home Page*, www.spss.com (accessed August 12, 2003).

3. P. Streifer, *Using Data to Make Better Educational Decisions* (Lanham, Md.: Scarecrow Education and AASA, 2002).

4. Pennsylvania Association of School Administrators, *Interpretive Guide & Technical Reference for the S&P School Evaluation Services*, www.pasa-net.org/www/index.html (accessed August 12, 2003).

5. Connecticut Department of Education, *Connecticut Mastery Test, Third Generation, Summary Performance Results, Grades 4, 6 and 8*, www.cmtreports.com (accessed August 12, 2003).

6. United States Department of Education, *United States Department of Education*, bco102.ed.gov/Programs/EROD/org_list_by_territory.cfm (accessed August 12, 2003).

7. T. Wagner and T. Vander Ark, *Making the Grade: Reinventing America's Schools* (New York: RoutledgeFalmer, 2001).

8. The College Board, *High School Grading Practices* (May 1998), www.collegeboard.com/research/html/rn04.pdf (accessed October 30, 2003).

Chapter Six

Welcome to the Test-Driven Accountability Era

INTRODUCTION

Clearly, in the eyes of both the Congress and Bush administration, the American educational system has failed to meet the needs of all students. To have come to this conclusion, they must believe that most past reforms have failed. Even the Clinton administration was an advocate of test-driven accountability as the roots of what became No Child Left Behind (NCLB) began in the late nineties. The result is NCLB—a strong and potentially illegal federal intrusion into state and local school governance. NCLB, at the minimum, is an expression of dissatisfaction with past educational reform attempts on the part of both the political "elites" and the public in general. Whether for good or bad, NCLB is forcing the educational establishment to change.

The strategies of change enacted by NCLB, largely relying on the use of standardized tests and the measurement of schools—not students—were the only statistically defensible tactics open to the Feds in attempting to achieve this level of school-based accountability. At this juncture, a great many of the states lack the capacity to implement all of the components of the act, even if they desired to do so. Thus, it is an open question whether NCLB, in its current form, will survive the next reauthorization.

Regardless, the bipartisan support that this act garnered is a clear expression of dissatisfaction with the public school system by Congress and the administration. And while it is probably too late to stave off the growing movement of charter schools, vouchers, and some of the sanctions imposed by NCLB on habitually failing public schools, such as providing parents more choice, applying the principles of data-driven decision making (DDDM) to identify and help underachieving students improve may be the education establishment's best hope to forestall some of the more draconian sanctions. At the least, that is the expectation. Whether DDDM as a tool for improvement can succeed is an open question due in large part to the nature of this work and the inherent limits of testing.

This new test-driven accountability era marks an end to the governance structure we have known over the past fifty years. The political elites, no doubt, are reveling in their success at finally breaking apart the lock hold the educational establishment has had on reforming the system. Those within the system, especially in urban schools, are almost working under a siege environment because of the new politics of reform. What we know for sure is that schools are now being judged through only one basic measure—standardized test scores. Consequently, we are in the era of test-driven accountability. For those seeking fundamental reform of the system, this "sea change" holds great promise. For many working within the system, however, this change portends calamity. Thus, depending on one's orientation, No Child Left Behind is either panacea or pariah.

There is growing concern that the law is flawed, too flawed to work. The National Council of State Legislatures has argued that the law represents another huge unfunded mandate on state and local government. And it is likely that increasingly more states will try to overturn several provisions of the act in the coming years or try to skirt the law altogether by not accepting ESEA funds. As of this writing, some fourteen states either have passed or have pending legislation to mitigate or seek waivers for those provisions they are unable to implement due to lack of capacity (human and material resources). However, it is unlikely that the Congress will make sweeping legislative changes in the act while there remains widespread bipartisan support for the goals of the law. Thus, No Child Left Behind is likely to be around for some time to come, although some of its more draconian provisions will likely be modified.

No Child Left Behind currently is the law of the land and, at the very least, it is useful to ask how it came to be that the federal government, which has no direct constitutional authority over public schools, now wields such fundamental power over the states and local school boards. The Tenth Amendment cedes responsibility for any function not specified in the

Constitution to the states—such as education, albeit there is a provision in Section 8 that could be construed to allow the federal government to intervene; it states, "The Congress shall have power to . . . provide for the common Defense and general Welfare of the United States."

Certainly, this level of federal control could not have come to pass without the consent of Congress and the desire of the people they represent. Those who view NCLB as a panacea argue that the public schools, especially the urban schools, have left millions of students behind. But those who work in these same schools argue that educators cannot meet the needs of such needy students with already limited resources. While insiders would probably not argue that these children are at a disadvantage, they do not believe that more student testing is the answer. But that may be the very point, that the purpose of NCLB is not just a student-testing program, but a lever for fundamental, sweeping change designed to force parents' options while breaking down traditional educational structures and controls over school governance.

If nothing else, NCLB has created a frenzy of activity and interest in data-driven decision making. Yet, as we have seen in earlier chapters of this book, DDDM is very hard work. And while there is some evidence that effectively implementing DDDM practices can bring about better decisions, there is no convincing evidence that DDDM alone results in improved student achievement. Educational organizations are just too complex to assume that a single process will result in meaningful and sustained change. I view DDDM as a necessary but insufficient condition for reform. The principles of DDDM are based on the heritage of program evaluation, total quality improvement, and systems thinking. Thus, there is some hope that focusing on student achievement may have long-term positive effects—even if one's orientation is that NCLB is a pariah.

Several key questions come to mind that will be explored in this chapter.

- We have been through *A Nation at Risk*, Goals 2000, and now No Child Left Behind—what is different and will it work? What impact will the limits of testing have on this agenda? What have been some recent abuses?
  - —Testing is driving much of the reform we see in schools today. What are the implications of test-driven reform on school improvement?

How can tests be used positively and how can the limits of testing be mitigated in the decision-making improvement process?
—What are the flaws in year-to-year, grade-to-grade level comparisons as required by NCLB, as opposed to following a cohort of the same students over time? What value can doing year-to-year assessment have?

- Given the hard work and sophisticated technology that DDDM requires, what are the implications on our expectation that accountability-driven reform will succeed?
- What are the national, state, and local policy implications?

HOW DID THINGS GET SO BAD? WHOSE SCHOOLS ARE THESE ANYWAY?

The federal Constitution cedes responsibility for education to the states, so how is it that Congress passed No Child Left Behind—the most significant federal intrusion into public education governance in history? Of course, the simple answer has to do with resources; Congress tied compliance to a huge federal grant program, ESEA—Title I. But there's something more at work here as the mood of the country is turning against the educational establishment, otherwise this level of federal intrusion would not be tolerated.

About a year ago, just when the true impact of NCLB was becoming clear, I knew of several Connecticut superintendents who seriously planned on either forgoing ESEA aid to skirt the impact of the law or, at the least, consolidating ESEA funds into fewer schools, as only ESEA schools were subject to the law's sanctions. Then, the Connecticut State Board of Education adopted the state's federal plan for NCLB as our state's school improvement program, mandating that all schools and districts "follow the rules" (although only ESEA schools would suffer the NCLB sanctions). This decision truly surprised a number of Connecticut educators and is indicative of the national mood regarding educational progress (or the lack of it). Undoubtedly, thousands of children in Connecticut are being left behind—for whatever reasons. And, as noted by our past commissioner of education, his hope was that NCLB would force some meaningful change in at least the state's urban districts. Connecticut's problems are not unique, and we can see across the nation an attempt to address poor achievement through a program of federally mandated process controls and sanctions.

There are many who argue that the "failure" of public education is contrived, based on the inappropriate use of test scores to evaluate schools. In fact there are those who would blame educators themselves as the cause of this degradation of public confidence, alleging that we have failed to be honest about testing, pointing out its limitations for such school evaluation purposes.[1] At the very least, test scores need to be part of an overall assessment process that uses a host of measures to be valid (APA[2]). Part of the problem has been a lack of consensus among educational insiders as to what reforms will work and which cannot. For example, there is ongoing debate about whether we should have a stronger standards-based approach and whether we should test teachers. We debate "more is less" while Carnegie units remain entrenched in the national high school psyche—and so on. We can see this ongoing debate played out through *A Nation at Risk* to H.R. 1804 Goals 2000 the Educate America Act[3] to the meeting of the nation's governors in Palisades, New York, in 1996.[4]

Moreover, the limitations of testing can confuse or mask deeper problems. For example, Hannaway argues that one essential dilemma may be with the schools' control structures, which are masked by the already cited problems with performance assessments. She concludes that,

> As a consequence, it is possible to conclude that accountability policies do not work in education, perhaps because of the federal structure or because of agency problems and education polecats, when in fact it is because the performance measures are faulty. Similarly, we could misdiagnose technical problems associated with performance measurement, not recognizing that the problem is a structural one or political one.[5]

There are also more esoteric arguments about the problems associated with understanding what test data tell us. For example, English[6] argues that most data (test scores) are not transformational; that is, we cannot learn enough from them to design meaningful decisions given the inherent complexity of schools.

Jennings[7] reviews much of the history of reform efforts, chronicling the growing role of the federal government in public education from President George Herbert Walker Bush to President George W. Bush to the enactment of NCLB. It becomes apparent through the debate over standards and accountability during the 1990s—which had little or no impact on the essential nature of schooling—that, as a result, Congress was ready for radical intervention. In another review of the social forces working against school reform, Greenberg[8] posits an impending "train wreck" due to the competing forces at work and the education establishment's inability to extricate itself from the current conundrum.

The growing federal role in public education is not a phenomenon of the late nineties but has been growing in intensity for the past fifteen years or more (see Boyd,[9] Jennings,[10] Kohlmoos,[11] Goertz[12]). This is a result of the widely held belief that the public school system is not working and fundamentally flawed.[13] Even if this consensus is wrong, that public education is working, such an argument has not been made persuasively by those who have attempted to set the record straight (see Boyd[14] and Troy[15]).

The perception that the schools are not working may go deeper than just student performance; it may be rooted in the liberal ideology of secularism as practiced by public schools (regardless of the constitutional requirement of separation of church and state). Boyd[16] argues that the nation's educational system is suffering from both a crisis in performance (poor children do, in fact, perform worse than wealthy children), that past reforms, no matter how well intentioned, simply have not worked, and a crisis of legitimacy—that schools are not seen as reflecting the beliefs of society. Boyd explains: "the perception remains that the public schools are highly secularized and not just neutral but hostile toward religious beliefs." (This is due, in part, to the ideology of public schooling and of public school teachers and teaching.) "In this context, and in view of accelerating controversies in the educational sector, it is clear that the politics of education is intensifying as the multicultural and rapidly changing aspects of our society become more obvious. Put another way, there is less social consensus, more 'pluribus' than 'unum,' and the 'one best system' approach to public education has collapsed along with the 'myth of the universal community'. In this new American society, many perplexing questions arise. What are our shared values? Whose history and 'common school' is it now, anyway? What should be the curriculum and character of public schools for the emerging 'new' America? Which of the many solutions being proposed should be adopted?"[17]

It may be that the very point of NCLB is to serve as a political lever to force change, any change, from the current one-size-fits-all, monopolistic system of American public education. Is Greenberg[18] right?—is this the "train wreck" public education is headed toward? After all, even if one accepts the arguments for using testing in the manner mandated by the law, the conclusion that not all children can succeed under the current system is inescapable. We know that poor achievement is closely related to poverty, changing family structures and parent's educational level—factors well beyond a school's control (see Biddle,[19] Grissmer et al.,[20] and Rothman[21]). Thus, how can *all* of the nation's schools succeed in leaving no child behind when so many external factors are outside their direct control? They probably cannot and alternative options will likely come onto the scene in greater numbers.

NCLB: FUNDAMENTALLY FLAWED OR GENIUS?

Everything we know about the appropriate use of standardized testing argues that NCLB is fundamentally flawed and will never work. Or will it? Another view posits that the framers created legislation that is more genius than folly. While the limits of standardized testing are well known and documented, it appears that NCLB gets it more right than wrong on this issue.

Riede[22] discusses the various problems associated with high-stakes tests. The uses and limits of testing are further explicated by Heubert and Hauser[23] in the report of the Committee on Appropriate Test Use, which lays out a host of recommendations to ensure that students are not unfairly hurt by the misapplication of high-stakes tests. In this comprehensive review, the commission asserts that tests should not be used singularly as the measures for high-stakes decisions, such as graduation, retention, and promotion.

Because testing is not well understood, it can be misused. The RAND Corporation[24] asserts that tests were being used to give education a "bad rap" through the reform debate and that the noneducational influences on achievement had not as yet been pinpointed by research. They noted "three kinds of misuse that should be avoided in honest, future debate":

> (1) simplistic interpretations of performance tests: these trends should not be taken at face value, ignoring the various factors that influence them (for example, demographic changes in tests takers or inflation of scores caused by test-based accountability); (2) unsupported "evaluations" of schooling: simple aggregate scores are not a sufficient basis for evaluating education—unless they provide enough information to rule out non-educational influences on performance. (Most test-score databases do not offer that kind of information); (3) a reductionist view of education: . . . education is a complex mix of successes and failures, what works in one context or for one group of students may fail for another.

If tests are going to be used for school improvement, there is a more appropriate way to proceed. NCREL,[25] drawing on the work of Hills,[26] notes that any serious (program) evaluation effort must match the purpose of the evaluation to the type of assessments needed for that purpose. They argue that to assess teaching and children's progress appropriately, one needs to use both formal assessments (appropriate criterion-referenced achievement tests) along with informal assessments (teacher-made tests and procedures, observation, analyses of work samples).

Popham[27] argues that standardized achievement tests are misnamed; that they do not measure what we think they measure—what students have learned in school. Rather, they are designed to measure differences across students. There are rather strict development rules for creating these tests to ensure test validity (does the test measure what it is intended to measure?) and test reliability (does the test produce the same results over multiple administrations?) (see Dietel[28] and National Forum on Assessment[29]).

Even if we were to resolve these thorny issues, Marzano[30] reminds us that "measurement experts now contend that anywhere from 10 to 36 performance tasks are necessary to assess accurately students' competence within a single subject area. Standardized tests utilize, typically, only six to eight items per subject area. In simple terms, (to perform well on tests) a district must teach to the specific content in the performance tasks and traditional test items that are used to determine whether students have met performance standards."

Webb[31] lists the quantitative and qualitative measures typically collected and used by schools to measure success, arguing that meaningful program evaluation requires more data input than simply using standardized test scores. Rorrer, too, notes that "multiple perspectives are necessary to provide a representative landscape of our individual and institutional ability to build and sustain the capacity for equity. . . . Proxies for educational equity must move beyond the existing reliance on standardized test scores and dropout rates to be inclusive of other measures."[32] Then there is the challenge posed by the current level of educator's skills for performing this work, as Stiggins points out—that teachers are not prepared for the "increasingly complex assessment challenges they face in the classroom."[33]

Since one of the main purposes of NCLB is to close the achievement gap, given all of the aforementioned challenges, the question remains whether testing students more will be successful. MacDonald and Shibles[34] argue that in order to close the achievement gap, two fundamental changes need to take place. First, the governance structure of schools needs to give principals real autonomy and authority. Second, complete school change is needed and several successful strategies are suggested. However, as we have already discussed, these proposed changes in governance have been debated for years with no real progress so far. Thus, one must ask whether NCLB is an attempt to cut through this political deadlock via test-driven accountability? At the very least, the result is some loss of local control, not more local autonomy on the major issues. Sergiovanni notes: "In today's environment, control over what is taught, how it is taught and what is learned is being increasingly transferred from parents, teachers and local citizens in the schoolhouse to legislators and other elites in the state house."[35] However, principals can still get this work done, as MacDonald and Shibles point out, if they have real authority over implementation.

WHAT HAPPENS WHEN SCHOOLS FOCUS ON TESTS?

Rabinowitz[36] argues that the use of more state-mandated assessments crowds out local assessments that are needed for a clearer picture of overall student growth. Kaufhold[37] notes that teaching to tests has eight significant undesirable effects: Doing so invalidates the test, promotes convergent thinking, promotes learning information that may be obsolete, excludes the arts and extracurricular activities, excludes the affective domain, overlooks discovery learning and promotes didactic instruction, involves only short-term memory, and excludes higher-order thinking skills. Sergiovanni states that, "When tests are the only determiner of future educational choices or future life choices, society tends to treat test results as the goal of schooling rather than as an indicator of achievement."[38] While NCREL notes that, "The primary strengths of standardized tests, if they are properly designed and properly used, are that they can eliminate biases in assessment of individual children and that they provide data that can be aggregated, permitting comparison of groups to a standard."[39]

Madaus[40] discusses the principles of testing, arguing that tests can have a limiting effect on what is taught and that standardized tests should be used for making comparisons across groups of students against a standard, not to measure individual student growth. This issue is best summed up by Wiggins, in November 1993, who notes that "The simplest way to sum up the potential harm of our current tests is to say that we are not preparing students for real, 'messy' uses of knowledge in context—the 'doing' of a subject. Or, as one teacher expressed it to me a few years ago, 'The trouble with kids today is that they don't know what to do when they don't know what to do.' That is largely because all our testing is based on a simplistic stimulus/response view of learning."[41]

Little has changed ten years after Wiggins wrote this, other than the fact that we are actually using more of these tests more often, not fewer or less often, to measure *school performance*. And that is the very point of NCLB—it does not pretend to measure student growth; the tests we are using today are just not designed for such a purpose. However, *they are* designed to aggregate student performance into groups to be compared against standards. The standards are the content of the tests, and the groups are the schools. Thus, if your orientation is to measure student growth over time, then NCLB is flawed. But if your essential purpose is to compare schools against a standard, NCLB is genius legislation (the complexities inherent within the actual implementation of the provisions of the act aside).

Why measure schools by grade level, year by year, rather than at the very least looking at how a cohort of students performs over time? The answer to this issue is easier to explain—it is a simple matter of the costs associated with test construction.

In order to measure a group's growth over time, let's say from grade four to five to six in reading, you must first clearly identify objectives to measure and then closely align them from year to year. Second, you must make certain that the content assessed is measured with common score types that are directly comparable. Third, be sure that there are enough and sufficient items/responses to measure what you are expecting to measure. And you must design a reliable test. Accomplishing all of this is expensive. Most tests in current use do not meet all of these requirements.

Short of this standard, Rothstein[42] shows that we cannot fairly and accurately compare test scores from the past to the present, or across different tests. Some of the challenges of doing this work were discussed in earlier chapters of this book, particularly in chapter 5, where we tried to make the best of available data to perform longitudinal and other studies.

Creating tests that meet these standards is feasible but extremely costly, and the framers of NCLB knew that standardized tests are not designed for such closely coupled analyses. Thus, the only thing left to do was to craft legislation that required assessment of the same grade level, year to year, so that the test does not change—the students do. This is also in keeping with the essential nature of standardized tests, that is, testing aggregate groups (grade levels in this case) against similar aggregate groups (the same grade level next year, and the following year, and so on).

WILL IT WORK?

We need to ask will this work? Will NCLB have any chance of succeeding at its fundamental goals of improving the achievement of underperforming children? Popham argues that it could if states were to utilize instructionally sensitive tests; that is, tests that are able to "assess students' mastery of a modest number of genuinely significant skills in reading and mathematics."[43] He notes that states have unfortunately selected the use of instructionally insensitive tests that are "incapable of detecting improved student learning, even if learning is present."

What is an example of an instructionally insensitive test? Popham states it is "any of the nationally standardized achievement tests that, in order to produce the score-spread required for their norm-reference comparisons, invariably contain too many items linked to students' socioeconomic status or inherited academic aptitudes. Such tests measure what students bring to school, not what they learn there."

Another challenge with NCLB has to do with where each state sets the benchmark for proficiency and the methods by which adequate yearly progress is measured from year to year. Because of the variability with which states have approached this issue, some states are identifying many more of their schools as failing than others. For example, in July 2002, there were no failing schools in Arkansas while there were 1,513 failing schools in Michigan. How can there be such a disparity? It depends on where each state sets its baseline for improvement and how large it determines each disaggregation subgroup must be. If the baseline is too low, fewer schools will initially fail. Similarly, if the disaggregation subgroup size is very large, very few schools will be noted as failing. And, of course, the corollary is also true: a higher baseline for proficiency and/or smaller subgroup sizes will yield more schools on the "in-need-of-improvement" list.

In Connecticut, state department officials examined these issues carefully, running a host of "what if" scenarios to find the right balance so that enough of the poorer-performing schools (in their view) were identified as failing but not so many as to be embarrassing for the state or to raise concerns over the law's legitimacy. Connecticut did well in this exercise and the actual schools identified this past year (2002–2003) seem to be the right candidates. However, even in this case there were at least two normally high-performing middle schools on the improvement list because only one subgroup in each school underperformed.

Bacon,[44] writing in *Time* magazine, notes that "because of the law's inflexibility thousands of schools are not making the grade. . . . In Florida, only 408 of 3,177 did well enough this year, meaning thousands of schools there could be failing next year" when the sanctions are imposed. These problems could result in the public losing confidence in the law, parents becoming frustrated at having their schools improperly identified, or, worse, educators themselves losing confidence in the law's capability to promote meaningful improvement and turning away from yet another reform effort.

Finally, there is the problem of executive level accountability. McLaughlin[45] notes that there are several factors that impact executive level accountability, and one outcome of the past twenty years of reform may have been to unintentionally weaken the authority of school leaders just when local authority needs strengthening. Factors that lead to a weakened accountability system that are related to education include: (1) the number of "actors" involved in decisions, (2) more decisions are made by groups, and (3) decisions are more open to impute and debate. Almost any important decision in a school today generates a great deal of debate by parents, teachers, the community leadership, and courts. This is one of the reasons why MacDonald and Shibles[46] argue that to effectively close the achievement gap, first and foremost, the governance model needs to be changed to give principals real authority over their programs. Murphy[47] contends that the administrative and bureaucratic structure of schools today is "incapable of meeting the needs of the public education system in the twenty-first century."

So, will NCLB work? Obviously, we do not yet know, but for the first time schools are being held accountable to a measurable standard, even if that standard is flawed as a gauge of student growth. This model of accountability yields winners and losers. Given the already bleak mood of the country regarding its confidence in public education, adding more negative press on top of what has come since *A Nation at Risk*, we can only assume that the spiral will continue downward.

It is likely, therefore, that NCLB will have at least one outcome, whether intended or unintended, labeling thousands of public schools as failing, thereby further degrading the nation's confidence in the institution. If those failing schools can improve, there is a chance that confidence can be restored. But the road ahead will not be easy given the ever-increasing demands and higher yearly standards mandated by "adequate yearly progress." Thus, even the states that initially set low benchmarks will soon start to feel the pressure unless the law is changed. Consequently, it may be that the lever sought by the political elites to reconstitute public education has been found and implemented.

On the other hand, if one believes that the lion's share of schools that have been identified truly do have underperforming students, then designing effective interventions can have a positive effect. On the belief that this goal is achievable, there are implications for data-driven decision making and state and local policy.

WHAT NOW? HOW DO WE PROCEED?

Simply identifying which schools are failing and which students are contributing to that condition will not be very useful. We need to drill down to search for relationships among performance and input data to help expose what specific areas of learning require intervention, for which students, and what programs are most likely to succeed at intervention. These steps require activity at Stages II and III, as discussed in earlier chapters. And because of the many problems associated with standardized tests, more specific and appropriate measures of student performance will be needed to help design meaningful interventions. Short, Short, and Brinson[48] present a useful schema for collecting a wide range of information that would be needed to make sound decisions—well beyond test scores. They also review the statistical functions needed to make these decisions, raising in our minds the challenge of professional development.

Bringing about change is not easy work. It requires capacity building—investing in the people who do the work to improve their knowledge and skill sets. It also requires providing the structural supports to help them get the work done. The proliferation of decision-support technologies, as discussed in chapter 2, are examples of structural supports. Providing training on the proper use and interpretation of test scores, for example, is capacity building.

But school improvement is even more complicated than this, as meaningful change requires effective local leadership that works on a foundation based on systems thinking and the recognition that systems are totally interrelated with one another, yielding often unintended outcomes requiring flexibility as the enterprise moves towards a common goal.[49] Supporting this point, Garmston and Wellman[50] note that school improvement requires an understanding of systems and their interrelatedness. They observe that school improvement is a complex task, requiring multiple sources of information and, even then, the outcomes are not guaranteed.

Program evaluation is also not a precise science. Hernandez[51] explains that one problem with evaluation is that most strategies "fail to account for essential information apart from the outcomes, which could later allow the agencies/programs to interpret and utilize the resulting information." He argues that when there is alignment among these essential data with outcome-relevant information, then effective evaluation is possible. As noted throughout this chapter, the measures used by NCLB are almost exclusively outcome measures. Thus, we need to incorporate a range of different data elements when exploring student achievement, and data warehouses are a good vehicle for facilitating this breadth of analysis.

There has been no shortage of debate on how to improve schools. The total quality movement was largely unsuccessful, in my view, because educators mostly forgot to include the high levels of analysis needed to make that effort work. Siegel and Byrne[52] observe that TQM requires both process and the analysis of quantitative measures to be successful.

There are those who argue that certain reform models are effective at positively influencing instructional practices, especially for children from low-income schools.[53] The belief that teachers can make a difference is further supported by Haycock,[54] who cites work done in Tennessee and Texas to show that the cumulative effects of teachers matter. Thompson[55] reviewed the various reform strategies employed in six cities, identifying common factors across all six sites. For example, the issue of whether leadership and authority are centralized vs. decentralized did not seem to matter—perhaps because, as McLaughlin[56] noted, still too many actors are involved in the essential decision making (of staffing, assignments, funding and allotments, etc.). Addressing the politics of reform, Thompson states, "But whether reform can be sustained (in these six cities) where all parties are not findings ways to work together remains doubtful."

Wagner[57] suggests an alternative to reform—the reinvention of schools "instead of focusing on stuffing kids' heads with more chemistry elements, history facts, math formulas and so on. The 'best practice' school increasingly takes a merit-badge approach to demonstrating mastery of vital competencies . . . workplace competencies, citizenship competencies, competencies for lifelong learning and competencies for personal growth and health." The real question is whether schools will have the time to focus on the proactive side of schooling, as opposed to constantly reacting to the demands and sanctions of NCLB and dealing with local politics. In at least one New York district that embraced Wagner's work, much of the initial reform effort stalled due to local political infighting over whether a corporate foundation was intruding upon schools too much.

To summarize the current state of reform and how to move forward, Elmore states:

> We are a knowledge-based enterprise, but, we have none of the characteristics of investment in human resources, attention to management and improvement, and resource allocation in the interest of performance that other knowledge-based organizations in our society have. We are totally out of sync with what is going on in the management of human resources in other sections, and we have a lot of catching up to do. That is part of the signal that this policy system is sending us. It is not just politicians; it is also the business community and, to some degree, the public.[58]

Elmore then outlines four aspects of the practice of improvement:

> The first is a relentless, tireless, and obsessive focus on the instructional core; (2) professional development and investments in knowledge and skill—how you should put the resources of the organization and the service of improving people's knowledge and skill into schools and classrooms; (3) an accountability system that is working functionally and effectively and; (4) having a coherent strategy for improvement.

So, what is next? Education must become serious about capacity building through professional development. It must provide the structural supports for educators to improve their skills and be as efficient as possible in doing this work. Thus, there are several recommendations that flow from this policy analysis.

RECOMMENDATIONS

- The federal government should revise the NCLB act to require that each state set as its baseline achievement level some common national percentile ranking. Doing so would make for comparisons that are more reasonable across states and school districts. While NAEP does achieve the goal of determining how well children do as compared to other nations and across states, NAEP results are not being used in the same way as NCLB testing. Thus, to level the playing field across states, but also to allow states the freedom to continue to select their accountability measures, a common standard should be established with regard to the baseline level of achievement, for example, the 65th national percentile. The federal government should also establish national uniformity regarding the cell sizes required for group disaggregations.

- States should provide resources to local districts to help them provide meaningful professional development in the interpretation and use of standardized tests, and their state improvement plans should mandate that local districts collect and analyze a range of data, in addition to standardized tests scores, in their program evaluation and improvement planning efforts. Moreover, financial assistance should be provided to local districts to acquire the appropriate decision-support technologies that will allow local educators to do this work efficiently. And since NCLB is essentially an unfunded federal mandate on states and local school districts, more federal dollars need to accompany the provisions of the act.
- Local school districts must develop a range of data that they regularly review internally to determine if schools are meeting their improvement goals—not relying solely on published annual state standardized test scores. Supervising, for example, teachers' and administrators' abilities to properly interpret test scores and relate such difficult concepts to parents such as why their son received an "A" in class but was "only" at the 70th national percentile, as this is an important measure of internal capacity. Other measures, such as the percent of meaningful parent involvement in the schools, the number of students participating in extracurricular activities, and so on, are all important measures of school success. School districts also need to adopt policies that ensure the proper and fair use of test data, such as prohibitions against using standardized tests scores as the main proxy for teacher effectiveness or student placement. Finally, school districts need to recognize that the work of data-driven decision making, made more necessary now due to NCLB, is hard to do and time consuming. To accomplish this work effectively, educators are going to need the proper time, technology, and training.
- K–12 educators need to recognize that the time for debate about national testing is over and that serious sanctions are about to be go into effect. The most serious sanctions will probably be first imposed just after publication of this book (spring/summer 2004). Educators need to explore why some students underperform and, to the extent that variables are under their control, make changes that are needed. Failing to

do so will more likely result in a growing charter school movement, not a return to the monopolistic era of the 1970s when educators were more solidly in control of schooling. They also need to learn the language of data-driven decision making and the new literacies required. There is no guarantee of success, but failing some forward movement, what is likely is more, not less, federal control and intervention.

SUMMARY

The past several years have brought about major changes in how schools are governed and managed. Control has systematically shifted from local educators and school boards to the state and political elites in Washington. Because education has largely been perceived as a failure over the last quarter century or more, Congress enacted the most intrusive test-driven accountability measure feasible to embarrass schools into improvement and, failing that, to close or reconstitute them, allowing for broader use of charter schools, giving students the right to attend more successful schools within a district.

Whether one supports the use of standardized testing for school accountability seems to be moot. And while it is almost certain now that some changes will be enacted in the law, what is most interesting and revealing is that very few in the nation argue against the fundamental target and goal of the law. Thus, some form of test-driven accountability and federal control is likely to continue. And this may be the true goal of NCLB, to break the establishment's stronghold of control on school reform, which has only led to deadlock, at least as viewed by the political elite.

Thus, we are left with one of two choices: (1) accept the challenge the law presents and attempt to make systemic changes aimed at improving the achievement of underperforming students, or (2) ignore the law, which would more likely result in continued federal and state intrusion and control. For those who choose to accept the challenge, there are a host of capacity-building tasks ahead. And, like so many other organizational problems, little can be accomplished without effective leadership—a topic to be addressed in the final chapter.

NOTES

1. W. J. Popham, *The Truth About Testing* (Alexandria, Va.: Association for Supervision and Curriculum Development, 2001).

2. *American Psychological Association*, Special Report on "Appropriate Use of High-Stakes Testing in Our Nation's Schools" (2003), www.apa.org (accessed September 12, 2003).

3. *Goals 2000: Educate America Act* (H.R. 1804), (Washington, D.C.: U.S. Government Printing Office, 1994).

4. *U.S. News*, Special Report on "The Battle over School Standards" (1996), www.usnews.com (accessed March 23, 1996).

5. J. Hannaway, "Accountability, Assessment, and Performance Issues: We've Come a Long Way . . . or Have We?" in *American Educational Governance on Trial: Change and Challenges*, ed. W. L. Boyd and D. Miretzky, 102nd ed. (Chicago: University of Chicago Press, 2003), 20–26, esp. 31.

6. F. W. English, "Dumbing Schools Down with Data-Driven Decision Making" in *The Postmodern Challenge to the Theory and Practice of Educational Administration*, ed. F. W. English (Springfield, Ill.: Charles C. Thomas, 2003), 201–10.

7. J. Jennings, "From the White House to the Schoolhouse: Greater Demands and New Roles" in *American Educational Governance on Trial: Change and Challenges*, ed. W. L. Boyd and D. Miretzky, 102nd ed., (Chicago: University of Chicago Press, 2003), 291–309.

8. A. Greenberg, "We Hold These Truths To Be Self-Evident: Why We Are About To Witness the Great American Education Train Wreck," *School Reform and the Superintendency* 5 (2003): 51–58.

9. W. L. Boyd, "Public Education's Crisis of Performance and Legitimacy: Introduction and Overview of the Yearbook" in *American Educational Governance on Trial: Change and Challenges*, ed. W. L. Boyd and D. Miretzky, 102nd ed. (Chicago: University of Chicago Press, 2003), 1–19.

10. Jennings, "From the White House to the Schoolhouse: Greater Demands and New Roles," 291–309.

11. J. Kohlmoos, "The Implications of ESEA Legislation," *School Reform and the Superintendency* 5 (2003): 41–49.

12. M. E. Goertz, "Standards-based Accountability: Horse Trade or Horse Whip?" in *From the Capitol to the Classroom: Standards-based Reform in the States*, ed. S. Fuhrman, 100th ed. (Chicago: University of Chicago Press, 2003), 39–59.

13. P. E. Peterson, ed., *Our Schools & Our Future . . . Are We Still at Risk?* (Stanford, Calif.: Hoover Institution Press, 2003).

14. Boyd, "Public Education's Crisis of Performance and Legitimacy."

15. F. J. Troy, "The Myth of Our Failed Education System," *The School Administrator* 55 (September 1998): 6–10.

16. Boyd, "Public Education's Crisis of Performance and Legitimacy."

17. Boyd, "Public Education's Crisis of Performance and Legitimacy," 12.

18. Greenberg, "We Hold These Truths To Be Self-Evident," 51–58.

19. B. J. Biddle, "Foolishness, Dangerous Nonsense, and Real Correlates of State Differences in Achievement," *Phi Delta Kappan*, www.pdkintl.org (accessed September 29, 1997).

20. D. W. Grissmer, S. Nataraj Kirby, M. Berends, and S. Williamson, *Student Achievement and the Changing American Family: An Executive Summary*: RAND, 1994 (also RAND research brief RB-8009).

21. R. Rothman, *Measuring Up: Standards, Assessment, and School Reform* (San Francisco: Jossey-Bass, 2000).

22. P. Riede, "Testing Dissidents," *The School Administrator* 58 (December 2001): 6–11.

23. J. Heubert and R. Hauser, eds., Committee on Appropriate Test Use. National Research Council (Washington, D.C.: National Academy Press, 1999). Also available at www.nap.edu.

24. RAND, "The Use and Misuse of Test Scores in Reform Debate—Policy Brief" (1994), RAND RP-278.

25. NCREL, "Strategies for Collecting, Recording, and Interpreting Assessment Information" (1997), www.ncrel.org.

26. T. W. Hills, "Reaching Potentials through Appropriate Assessment" in *Reaching potentials: Appropriate Curriculum and Assessment for Young Children*, ed. S. Bredekamp and T. Rosegrant, vol. 1 (Washington, D.C.: National Association for the Education of Young Children, 1992), 43–63.

27. W. J. Popham, "Standardized Achievement Tests: Misnamed and Misleading," *Education Week* (2001), www.edweek.org/ew/ewstory.cfm?slug=03popham.h21&keywords=Standardized%20Achievement%20Tests%3A%20Misnamed%20and%20Misleading.

28. R. J. Dietel, J. L. Herman, and R. A. Knuth, *What Does Research Say About Assessment?* (1991), www.ncrel.org (accessed October 29, 1997).

29. NCREL, *Standards for Technical Qualities* (1997), www.ncrel.org (accessed October 29, 1997).

30. R. J. Marzano, "Rethinking Tests and Performance Tasks," *The School Administrator* 55 (December 1998): 10–12.

31. F. Webb, "The Necessary Art of Program Assessment," *Thrust for Educational Leadership* 25 (February–March 1996): 30–32.

32. A. Rorrer, "Educational Leadership and Institutional Capacity for Equity," *UCEA Review* 43, no. 3 (2002): 1–5.

33. R. J. Stiggins, "Confronting the Barriers to Effective Assessment," *The School Administrator* 55 (December 1998): 6–9.

34. J. T. MacDonald and M. R. Shibles, *Closing the Achievement Gap* (Storrs, Conn.: The New England Center for Educational Policy and Leadership, Neag School of Education, University of Connecticut, October 2003).

35. T. J. Sergiovanni, "Standards and the Lifeworld of Leadership," *The School Administrator* 57 (September 2000): 6–12.

36. S. Rabinowitz, "Balancing State and Local Assessments," *The School Administrator* 58 (December 2001): 16–20.

37. J. Kaufhold, "What's Wrong with Teaching for the Test?" *The School Administrator* 55 (December 1998): 14–16.

38. Sergiovanni, "Standards and the Lifeworld of Leadership," 11.

39. NCREL, *Standardized Tests*, ncrel.org (accessed October 29, 1997).

40. G. F. Madaus, "The Influence of Testing on the Curriculum" in *Critical Issues in Curriculum*, ed. L. Tanner (Chicago: University of Chicago Press, 1988), 83–121.

41. G. Wiggins, "Assessment: Authenticity, Context, and Validity," *Phi Delta Kappan* 75, no. 3 (November 1993): 200–14.

42. R. Rothstein, "Skewed Comparisons," *The School Administrator* 55 (December 1998): 20–24.

43. W. J. Popham, "The 'No Child' Noose Tightens—But Some States Are Slipping It," *Education Week* 24 (September 2003): 48.

44. P. Bacon Jr., "Struggle of the Classes," *Time* 162 (September 22, 2003): 42–43.

45. D. J. McLaughlin, "Strengthening Executive Decision Making," *Human Resource Management* 34 (Fall 1995): 443–61.

46. J. T. MacDonald and M. R. Shibles, *Closing the Achievement Gap*.

47. J. F. Murphy, "Core Strategies for Reforming Schooling," *The School Administrator* 56 (December 1999): 20–21.

48. P. M. Short, R. J. Short, and K. Brinson Jr., *Information Collection The Key to Data-Based Decision Making* (Larchmont, N.Y.: Eye on Education, 1998).

49. P. A. Streifer, *Using Data to Make Better Educational Decisions* (Lanham, Md.: Scarecrow Education with the American Association of School Administrators, 2002).

50. R. Garmston and B. Wellman, "Adaptive Schools in a Quantum Universe," *Educational Leadership* 52, no. 7 (April 1995): 6–12.

51. M. Hernandez, *Using Logic Models and Program Theory to Build Outcome Accountability*, available from OCLC FirstSearch website, newfirstsearch.oclc.org (accessed July 25, 2001).

52. P. Siegel S. and Byrne, *Using Quality to Redesign School Systems* (San Francisco and Milwaukee: Jossey-Bass with ASQC Quality Press, 1994).

53. L. Skrla, "The Influence of State Accountability on Teacher Expectations and Student Performance," *The Review* 42, no. 2 (2001): 1–4.

54. K. Haycock, "Closing the Achievement Gap," *Educational Leadership* 58 (March 2001): 1–8.

55. S. Thompson, "All Means All—Part 2," *Strategies* 9, no. 1 (2002): 1–2.

56. McLaughlin, "Strengthening Executive Decision Making," 443–61.

57. T. Wagner, "Reasons to Learn in the New Village Schoolhouse," *The School Administrator* 56 (December 1999): 27–29.

58. R. F. Elmore, "Practice of Improvement," *School Reform and the Superintendency* 5 (2003): 23–39.

Chapter Seven

The Softer Side of Leadership

George Goens with Philip Streifer

School improvement is extremely challenging work. Schools are highly complex organizations with many interrelating systems. Building institutional capacity to accomplish this work will require more than just teaching the requisite skills. It will require extremely capable leadership. Within this context, the mantle of leadership is filled with responsibilities and obligations. Leaders face the undertow of change and exploding demands, all requiring leaders with skill, conceptual knowledge, refined interpersonal qualities, and strength of character to address complex issues creatively. The accountability requirements of test-driven reform are yet another force that must be channeled; data-driven decision making is worrisome for many educators because of all the new literacies required.

How do you lead schools through the maze of challenges they now face? What does effective leadership require in this new era? What does the environment look like? Recently the group of educators planning the Bill and Melinda Gates project in Connecticut worked on the problem of identifying what "whole school change" looks like and what the leadership demands are in this new organizational setting. Figure 7.1 demonstrates the complexity of today's schools in which there is no direct path to success, and the landscape is mired with challenges.

So how does one lead in this new environment of test-driven accountability? Surprisingly, we have found that it requires a special set of skills—a softer side of leadership—not what one might normally expect in a numbers-driven world. Thus, the purpose of this chapter is to explain what we mean by the softer side of leadership and how it can help build institutional capacity.

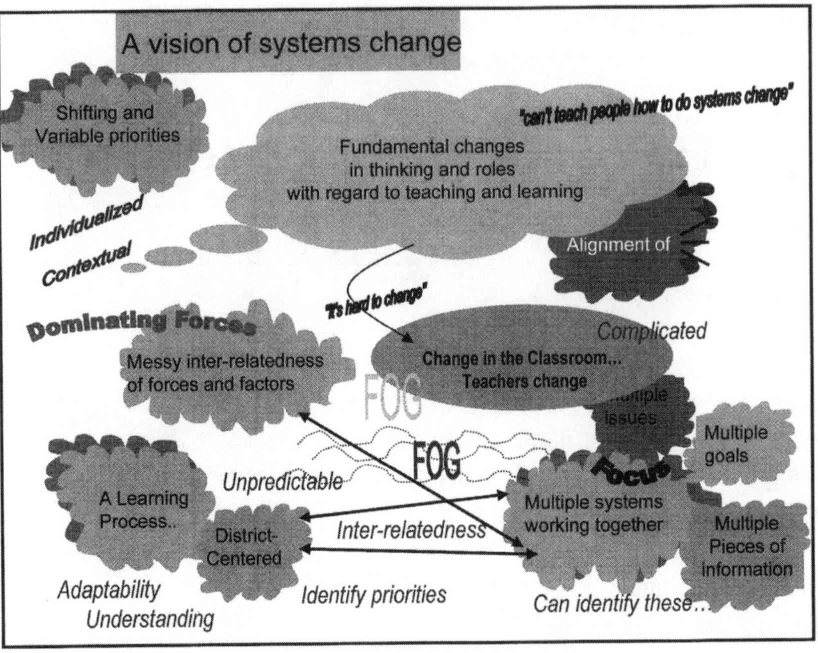

Figure 7.1. A Vision of Systems Change and the Role of Leadership

THE SOFTER SIDE OF LEADERSHIP

Leaders make decisions. Those decisions require substance and integrity if schools are to be successful. And information is the ground on which leaders stand in decision making. Without information, neither strategies nor substance will be implemented successfully. Having the information and acting on it does not represent, in and of itself, effective leadership. As we have said before: data-driven decision making is a necessary yet insufficient condition for successful improvement. Using data to make decisions in a poisoned environment can be more harmful than not using it at all in a neutral environment. Thus, there is a strong role for effective leadership.

Effective organizations are those where the energies of all within the enterprise are focused toward common goals. Information should put the organization "in-formation" to address challenges. Being "in-formation" simply means that goals are clear and outcomes and strategies are in harmony with the school's values, thereby focusing people's energy and commitment. In-formation is a matter of integrity and credibility.

Knowledge and information go hand in hand. The proper management of information is essential to applying knowledge to make essential strategic or substantive decisions. But not all knowledge is the same.

EXPLICIT AND IMPLICIT KNOWLEDGE

Knowledge comes in two forms—explicit and tacit. Explicit knowledge is what generally comes to mind when we think of knowledge because it can be written down or expressed in some tangible form. Explicit knowledge is shown in numeric analyses, facts, dates, events, or any other metrical form. It can be pulled from databases and analyzed.

Tacit or implicit knowledge, however, is different. It does not appear to be as "hard" as explicit knowledge in that it is not as measurable, tangible, or objective. Implicit knowledge takes the form of attitudes, expressions, feelings, or intuitive senses. Tacit knowledge is highly personable and harder to formalize. Its genesis is in relationships, interactions, and observations and develops into intuition, insights, and hunches. It often comes through experience and trusting and respecting our innate ways of learning. H. Ross Perot described intuition as simply "knowing your job" in manifest and subtle ways.

Logical reasoning and analysis are not the only ways we learn and gain knowledge. We synthesize data, feelings, emotions, energy, and other tangibles and intangibles in order to make sense of the world and to act. Sometimes tangible data and information miss the key links to success that are rooted in the intangibles of motivation, commitment, imagination, and creativity. "Hard" data does not often reflect the human side of enterprises. In this context, data-driven decision making can become a cold, matter-of-fact business. This may not sit well in a people-oriented industry because people must accept and act on the findings if schools are to improve.

Leaders work on a number of different planes in obtaining and applying both tacit and explicit knowledge. In one sense, explicit knowledge is part of the "doings" of leading and managing. The "doings" or actions involve the activities of planning, organizing, directing, reviewing, evaluating, analyzing, budgeting, and other management tasks. While leaders accomplish these things and rely on tangible information for many of these tasks, the intangibles may often concern the critical issues that define success or failure.

LEADERSHIP AND RELATIONSHIPS

The essence of leading is "being" in relationship. It is not just a bunch of tasks to be completed. It is more complicated and less tangible than that. In talent-driven organizations, relationships are primary, otherwise data, information, and knowledge will not be used to greatest effect. There are organizations with an abundance of data and information that are failing because of dysfunctional relationships that squander potential and talents.

In relationships, leaders must live in the present moment, show care for others, and respect others' gifts and promises. Leaders are to help others "complete themselves," in the words of Bill O'Brien, former president of Hanover Insurance Company and a central figure in Peter Senge's book *The Fifth Discipline*. There is no explicit road map for helping people "complete themselves" because each relationship is different and unique. Relationships can create energy for learning and development or its absence can stymie growth.

Leaders "being" in relationships must also be in harmony with the values of the organization and their own principles. Harmony has to do with integrity because relationships that do not mirror values are bankrupt and hollow. Credibility, which is the cornerstone of leadership, is based on integrity and leaders acting in accord with proper ethics and values.

In a sense, all relationships must be fractals. A fractal is a repeated pattern—each fractal is a smaller version of the whole. The leaves on a fern, for example, are smaller replicas of the larger plant. In this sense, every relationship and interaction the leader and others have in an organization must be a replica of the values and spirit of the larger organization and what it stands for. Any deviation from this model and the interaction lacks integrity and principle. Leaders who say, "Don't watch my actions, look at the results," eventually fall because they fail to live up to ideals.

RELATIONSHIPS AND POWER

Relationships based on integrity to principles and values create energy. The work of leadership is exercised through power and there are two types of power. One focuses on control and domination. The other involves energy and capacity. There is no equation for human energy. Leaders' relationships must produce the creative and imaginative energy to create commitment and revitalize the spirit of people and the organization.

Being a leader further involves creating a conversation and engaging in a dialogue about purpose and passion. Conversations and dialogues, based on mutuality and respect, provide a means for mutual understanding of direction and purpose and allow people to see how their calling connects with a greater purpose. It can provide a sense of efficacy. Leaders must be cognizant of the web of connections and interconnections in organizations and create a climate of innovation and commitment.

REALITY AND RELATIONSHIPS

If relationships are all there is to reality, as quantum physicists assert, then the nature and type of relationships leaders have is a central question. Knowledge—explicit or implicit—cannot be used and organizational capacity cannot be deepened if relationships are not mutual and respected. Dysfunctional relationships can "deep six" any amount of measurable data and information in the fog of distrust and fear. It is ironic that the intangibles of relationships, built on love, trust, commitment, or any other "soft" and difficult-to-measure quality, can disarm a mountain of data and logic.

A key issue is: What relationships are essential to leaders? A primary relationship is the one between leaders and themselves. "Know thyself" has been a mantra in leadership studies, but it is often given short shrift or ignored. For one thing, it is a difficult concept and, second, there is no recipe for knowing one's self. This relationship is frequently ignored, but leaders who are uncomfortable with themselves come across as disingenuous and phony.

In today's dynamic, accountability-driven environment, with multiple expectations and the demands for quick and measurable results, leaders can be consumed and fall out of balance. Maintaining balance—physical, emotional, spiritual, and intellectual—is essential if leaders are to develop positive relationships with others. A strange and unhealthy concept heard among leaders is that it is "lonely at the top." The notion of separation is destructive to creating trusting and genuine relationships. Separation is contrary to people's need for connection and sense of efficacy.

People long to be connected to others and to have a calling greater than themselves.

Balance is necessary for everyone. For people in jobs that can be all-absorbing, it is an essential, otherwise health deteriorates, behavior becomes barometric, and creativity evaporates. Leaders need to maintain emotional, physical, and spiritual balance. Being a workaholic who does not take vacations eventually destroys physical health, taxes emotions and creative energy, and harms family relationships that provide the love, acceptance, and security we all need.

If leadership requires passion for ideas and energizing and imaginative relationships, then leaders have to take care of themselves and understand what principles and values they hold dear. This is also an aspect of balance. Leaders need to understand their values and live in harmony with them. Otherwise, a gnawing discomfort and unrest will tear at their souls and result in growing dissatisfaction and disillusionment.

ON LEADERSHIP AND STEWARDSHIP

Leaders, especially the great ones, are true to their beliefs and values. They stand for noble causes and they "fight the good fight" with integrity even if failure is probable. Many urban educators are fighting the good fight today given the demands of No Child Left Behind, the achievement gap and its fundamental causes—poverty. Serving and reaching ideals presupposes that leaders recognize and commit to the ideals that are true to them. Inspiring leadership does not come from processes or data. It is borne in noble goals. You cannot mobilize support and commitment based on tactics and numbers. It takes passion and leadership that is value-driven to inspire leadership in others.

In schools, another primary relationship leaders have is with students. It is understood that children are at the center of education and schooling. But, losing sight of children and the sanctity of childhood can result as we "target" service, pursue measurable standards, integrate technology, and differentiate our strategies. Children have been dehumanized in some organizations to customers, clients, stakeholders, target audiences, and AYP numbers. They are categorized into ethnic groups, ability groups, quartiles, subgroups, remediation groups, and a phalanx of special education categories. In all this analysis of learning needs and groupings, we fail, at times, to address children as curious, creative, compassionate, and loving people. Reaching the next test level becomes primary and the less tangible aspects of education—character, imagination, and obligation—can get steamrolled.

In the process, we can produce children who are well schooled and poorly educated. Children require the same physical, emotional, and spiritual balance as adults. Too many seventy-five-pound children carry thirty-pound backpacks through a highly scheduled and pressured day, bombarded with electronic stimuli.

Finally, leaders are in relationship with people serving in the organization and those in the larger community, including teachers, staff, school board members, parents, and community members. While these relationships require respect and trust, they also must meet a higher test of obligation. Leaders have moral commitments that go beyond just "doing" the tasks necessary to meet their role description. Stewardship is an obligation all leaders face that comes from the desire to serve others, not control or manipulate them. Stewardship requires that leaders leave the organization in better shape than they found it. In the moral sense, then, leaders face the test of goodness, which requires that their leadership be founded in positive values and the principles of justice, equality, liberty, beauty, and truth, all of which are prerequisites for stewardship. Without stewardship, organizations can get lost in the mire of dishonesty and ego. Integrity between values and actions and between ends and means is essential to leaders as stewards. Pursuing noble goals through corrupt measures has no virtue. Using data and information for selfish or hollow goals lacks honesty and credibility.

Ego can also corrupt. Leading to enhance a résumé is self-centered and dangerous because it is contrary to leadership as service to others. In that regard, ego can create defensiveness, self-protection, and the desire for security, which erases the risks leaders need to take in addressing important issues of principle. The risk of leadership is standing up for principles and integrity no matter the personal hazards. Leadership is not a position of safety and self-aggrandizement. Stewardship requires courage, not security; it demands honesty, not ambiguity; it cries for passion, not politics.

To be a steward requires that leaders care for the resources and people in the organization. With physical resources, it is evident that they should be maintained. With people, however, we sometimes forget our role as stewards. Our role is not to cure people but to care for them. Caring is an act of affection for humanity, ambivalence is not.

Stewardship requires that, as leaders, we create a nurturing environment where individuals can use their talents and meet their potential in a cause greater than themselves. It is a matter of giving of yourself to help others meet their calling and find their place and a sense of efficacy. When people are in their element, they can gracefully complete their work and find satisfaction and commitment.

When this happens, the organization increases its ability to serve. Creativity and imagination can be applied to the difficult problems of schools and children. The leaders, then, model the behavior and passion that should be applied to caring for children and their needs so they can develop the bundle of energy and potential they were born with and go on to leading lives of goodness and integrity.

The paradox in many books on leadership is that relationships are described in military terms as if they were carried out on battlefields. Language of tactics and strategies, such as "media blitzes," "rallying the troops," "taking no prisoners," and "falling on swords," are frequently used. Caring, in these contexts, seems weak and ineffectual; serving seems wimpish when prevailing at all costs is the language of the day.

Serving is not free of conflict, but it is not a battlefield exercise. It includes working with people and creating a crucible in which they learn, grow, and use their creativity and imagination. It requires an environment of respect, compassion, forgiveness, empathy, and understanding. Our mythology extols hard-driving and hard-line leaders. But allowing people to be creative means that they have a voice, and that can be unsettling to leaders who are cloaked in a mantle of control. Appearing soft, in this view, is a recipe for ineptness and failure.

The old connotations of "hard" and "soft" leaders need to be erased, because addressing the soft issues is one of the hardest roads a leader can take. Soft leadership is *not*:

- Indecisiveness
- Meekness
- Fearfulness
- Avoidance of problems with people, finances, or substantive direction

- Sappy emotionalism
- Weakness
- Illogical or mushy thinking
- Shrinking in the face of crises

In life, it seems, paradox is our companion. The same is true with the terms "soft" and "hard" when it comes to leadership. It is harder to be soft, and it is easier to be hard. Being uncompromising, tough, and directing is the easiest form of management because you strictly follow regulations and do not expose yourself as a human being. You simply play a role and focus on consistent processes and superordinate controls and regulations.

Making people tow the mark is easy, particularly if you have the ability to impose retribution and punishment. Either by errors of omission (not knowing better) or errors of commission (purposeful misuse), data-driven decision making can too often be used destructively. Driving and pushing people is not a difficult act: it may be frustrating, but it is not difficult. And for short bursts of time, people may be moved in a particular direction by this approach and show increases in performance.

"Hard" leaders can move people, but they may not motivate them. Working from fear drives out the love people have for their work and for the organization. Fearful people may be moved to do something in the face of power or control, but they will not commit and be motivated to go beyond the defined request. They don't add their creativity or innovativeness to the solving of problems. "Tough" leaders who operate from a "you don't have to like it, you just have to do it" framework, leave the organization sapped of pride and passion.

So-called "soft" leaders, who work from understanding, compassion, and commitment to stewardship, are concerned with wholeness and integrity. When things are disharmonious, a leader does not break the spirit or damage the talent in the system. Schools run on talent and talent should not be intimidated out of people. Creative people will turn their talents on beating the system, not enhancing it. That is why creating a compassionate and caring environment is so important.

The intangibles, or soft side of leadership, are wrapped in our relationships with ourselves and with others. Facing issues with pride and passion comes from within us, as individuals, and from the groups we work with. Destroying a relationship has repercussions throughout the organization.

Tough leaders may get immediate action but cause the organization to wither and die in the long term because cancerous conduct depletes motivation and will. Short-term movement is a big price to pay at the expense of long-term growth and learning.

Soft leadership is something else. It requires the biggest risk a leader can take—exposing oneself as a real person in an authentic way, complete with one's vulnerabilities and unique humanness. Softness involves being subtle, sensitive, flexible, open, approachable, and perceptive. It does not mean foisting emotions on people, being smarmy, or breaching the normal barriers of propriety we all maintain. But it does mean:

- Knowing yourself and being self-reflective
- Taking the risk to be yourself
- Understanding that leadership does not reside in one position or person
- Breaking barriers and artificial walls that separate people
- Being vulnerable as a leader, being "comfortable in your own shoes," and not role-playing
- Recognizing the ability of ordinary people to do extraordinary things
- Seeing connections and interrelationships between people and the natural order of things
- Recognizing that structures are more than roles—that they are also values, ethics, norms, and principles
- Seeing people as they are with ideas, emotions, gifts, and energy
- Understanding that everything that can be counted may not count in the greater order of things
- Knowing that the human spirit can be noble, creative, imaginative, and selfless

From this perspective, soft leadership can produce two bottom lines: results in terms of desirable outcomes and productivity, and strong connections and ties between people who long to belong to an enterprise in which they can use their talent to serve and to act as stewards of the common good. Some athletes are said to have soft hands. They can catch the hard throws or they can make shots that require finesse and sensitivity. Leaders need softness, too, to deal with the conflict and the complex challenges they face, as well as to create productive relationships with people.

RELATIONSHIPS AND CONFLICT

Conflict is not a bad thing, and neither is confusion, which often is conflict's companion. In fact, conflict is inevitable in life because life is not a place of equilibrium. In searching for homeostasis, conflict happens, change occurs, and energy is expended.

Leaders must sometimes create conflict if they act as stewards meeting their obligations. Conflict comes from a variety of sources and is created when:

- We require ourselves to do something painful
- We require others to do something they don't want to do
- We require each other to do what neither wants to do
- Other people want to do something we don't want them to do

Conflict and change can be painful. Sometimes pain has little to do with physical hurt. Many times it is the emotional pain of cutting programs that we developed that haven't produced results. Or, it is confronting people we like and respect with data that are negative or signaling that their behavior is incongruent with values and obligations. Pain comes from not having the skills to meet new challenges or adapt to change.

When people don't want to do things that contribute to a successful and positive environment, leaders must be a source of feedback and the gatekeeper of credibility and integrity. That feedback may hurt and cause concern. At times, both leaders and followers must face difficult choices. As stewards, there is great weight placed on the shoulders of professionals to do no harm and to address issues. Stewards do not belittle or damage potential and integrity. They are builders, not destroyers, and must "be" and "act" with integrity, passion, and commitment to principles.

In other situations, some individuals may head on a course that is contrary to principles and values or take positions of ego-driven self-interest and not consider the common good. Leaders then must confront the issues and help people return to projects, issues, and approaches that are in harmony with the school's values. Compassion means helping people, even if confrontation is necessary. The issue is how the confrontation is approached.

Conflict is not the issue in leadership—relationships are. How leaders behave in situations of conflict, how they act to preserve integrity of values, and how they enhance the potential and commitment of people are what is significant in leadership.

LEADERSHIP AND ATTACHMENTS

Ghandi believed that all leaders must know their attachments, otherwise they will succumb to them in subtle ways and compromise their principles. Attachments are the "relationships, possessions, privileges, and other components of our life we do not want to give up." Knowing yourself means knowing your attachments.

Leaders can be attached professionally to competence, status, power, and acceptance. On a personal level, they can be attached to status, money, geography, or image. Some of these attachments are conscious ones, and others may be subconscious. Discovering them, however, is essential; otherwise they can cloud judgment and decisions.

Attachments to power, privilege, and possessions can make integrity to principles difficult if we do not identify them. These attachments can create subtle confrontations with us. Do we risk jeopardizing an attachment to do the right thing? For example, many leaders are attached to competence—being perceived by others as capable and assured. Competence is demonstrated by success, and success leads to security. That is why some leaders and executives cannot admit a mistake or indicate a shortfall in reaching goals. Failure is anathema to people attached to always being right and having their self-image connected to recognized success and status.

Competence, success, and security are positive things in life. The issue is attachment. For example, if the data indicate that goals are not being reached and a leader's self-esteem or job security might be threatened, will he or she speak out and candidly report the data if they are attached to competence and security? There are examples in all sectors of life where data were stretched, false pictures were painted, issues were buried, or scapegoats were identified to protect a person's image.

People in danger of losing their power and authority will sometimes compromise principles and fall into self-protection, secrecy, or ducking responsibility. Attachments can obscure judgment and focus. Attachments create the crossroads where the soft issues of leadership—compassion, credibility, forgiveness, and understanding in relationships—meet the hard data and information that are some of the indicators of achieving goals and succeeding.

Wise leaders free themselves from their attachments. They are at peace with what happens from their best efforts. As a world of disequilibrium, there are forces—manifest and hidden—over which leaders have very little control. Those forces, plus the best-intentioned and planned initiatives or strategies, can lead to failure or falling short of expectations.

Being at peace with success or failure is not easy. It does not mean failure is accepted, it simply means that you are at peace with yourself in doing your best. In that regard, reporting it in the best interests of the organization and the children is an act of courageous leadership; it is not an act of weakness or incompetence.

Principles are not always tangible; they can be abstractions that are always in the process of being defined by events. For example, is it ever appropriate for a leader to lie? Some might say that the president should not be truthful to protect national security and our democracy. But others, Ghandi included, would argue that a president who lies weakens the very democracy he or she intends to protect because the people become untrustworthy of and cynical toward our government. Credibility is lost, and with it the ability to lead.

In this context, are the framers of No Child Left Behind correct in their assumptions about schooling? Have they gone too far in holding schools accountable for society's failures? Are we correct in assuming that being data driven can solve all of these problems? Some of these problems?

A leader's moral obligation is not to subordinate principles to the desire for success or to attachments. Virtue comes from adherence to principles in pursuit of success. This means that data and information are managed, analyzed, synthesized, evaluated, and presented honestly and ethically even if they jeopardize a leader's personal standing and attachments.

If this occurs, then the leader, organization, and community can continue to learn and search for the right answers. No one can succeed all the time. Falling short offers the opportunity, not only for growth, but also for creative problem solving and deepened commitment.

APPROACHES TO LEADERSHIP

Critical issues in leadership have to do with relationships and results. Leadership is not about "toughness"—controlling, manipulating, threatening, or aloofness. It really is about connections between people, between people and purpose, and between calling and fulfillment.

In leadership there are several key questions:

- What increases people's capacity to solve problems?
- What connects people?
- What nurtures creativity?
- What develops commitment?
- What generates motivation?
- What gets results?
- What really makes a difference?

Treating people as untrustworthy deviants will not address these questions long-term nor with lasting results because this creates distance between leaders and followers. The greater the distance people have from leaders, the less positive the results. The less distance there is from the leader, the more positive the results.

What is distance concerning leadership? It is the distance between:

- Words and behavior
- Values and processes
- Goals and outcomes
- Self and authenticity
- Experience and learning
- Relationships and significance
- Effort and success

Distance is also created when we value numbers more than people. Leaders who are "distant" lack passion and a sense of commitment to the people they lead, and treating people as interchangeable parts does not create respect and commitment. Distance between leaders and followers dooms an organization to failure.

People long for connection, not separation. They long for connection between their work and purpose, between people and cooperation, and between leaders and their aspirations. They do not yearn for leaders as vestiges of distant power or leaders more interested in material things than people and principle. Essentially, people want leaders who are human and approachable and who do not hide behind the façade of a title.

Motivation comes from efficacy and connection, both of which can pull an organization to higher levels of performance. Nurturing and closeness are keys to high performance. Seeing the wonder in human beings and providing an environment in which they can learn and contribute is a leader's obligation.

In our penchant to manage, we sometimes forget the corollaries to providing success and the major metric indicators. The paradox is that to produce tangible numbers, leaders must rely on the intangibles of imagination, creativity, spontaneity, synchronicity, serendipity, and joyful fun. High-performing, successful organizations have people with these qualities. They are not dour and humorless places that operate by highly regimented behavior long-term. There is little distance in these places between people and their passion and commitment.

LEADERSHIP AND DECISION MAKING

Leaders need to know how to improvise to reach goals and objectives. To survive in an ever-changing, unpredictable world, leaders must improvise, which requires two types of decisions. First are substantial decisions that concern destinations—the "whats" of goals and objectives. The second type of decision is about tactics or strategies—the processes and approaches to be used to reach the destination. Goals are dependent on the "hows"—strategies—in order to be realized.

Substantial and tactical decisions rely on logical, cognitive analysis as well as intuitive and affective ways of knowing. It is in this context that data-driven decision making, as presented in this book, has value and purpose. We have all been in situations where the data said one thing and we did another because it did not feel "right" or just did not "fit" our intuitive sense. Leaders must use all their ways of knowing in order to make both kinds of decisions in a chaotic and nonrational world. They adjust, "go with the flow," take a "half a loaf," and wait until "the time is right." Metrics can provide an analysis, but insight comes from coupling data with our other cognitive, intuitive, or affective ways of understanding our world.

Leaders are players—not in a manipulative or devious way, but in a positive manner. They look forward, not backward. They understand that although chaos in the world exists, they have choices and can respond. Because they may have created the dilemma, they accept responsibility and feel an obligation to find a solution. They have a sense of efficacy and are "response-able." They use their data, their relationships, and their intuition to make conscious choices and to respond. Leaders are mindful and aware, whereas victims wear the shawl of innocence and engage in blaming.

"SOFT" LEADERSHIP: THE ESSENCE OF AUTHENTICITY

Soft leadership is not weak leadership. It is not wishy-washy, "feel good" pseudo-psychological jargon. Soft leadership is about being committed and involved with your total faculties as a human being and creating relationships in which people can meet their potential in the face of difficult issues. In that regard, leaders face their obligations with their total being—with their head, heart, and spirit. Figure 7.2 presents the critical components of a leader who applies all of his or her dimensions to leading, not just linear analysis.

Certainly, leadership requires a keen intellect and a deep cognitive understanding of the substance of the work. Leaders need the ability to comprehend, analyze, synthesize, and evaluate tangible and intangible information. Intelligence and competence are skills essential to developing, sharing, and communicating a "vision" or direction. Leaders with the cognitive knowledge and skills to engage in a dialogue about schools and what they should be for children will be more successful than those who simply react to issues.

Knowledge and skills, however, are insufficient for true leadership. Morally corrupt endeavors can be carried out efficiently and effectively. Smart, talented people who produced and analyzed numbers efficiently

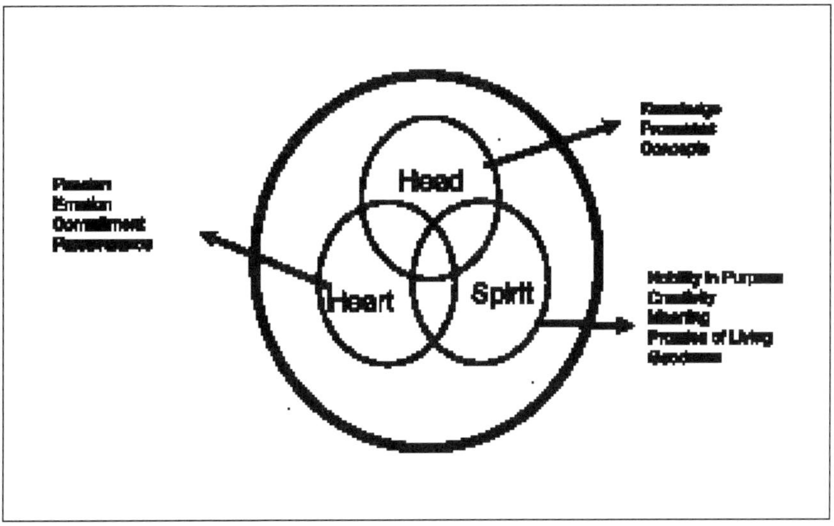

Figure 7.2. Leadership Model

led Enron and other failed corporations. Leaders need heart to pursue noble goals courageously in the face of daunting odds, and they need heart to risk, persevere, and challenge even if rational logic dictates otherwise. Overcoming odds, in the face of criticism from the majority, takes courage and peace of mind.

Second, heart addresses critical qualities of healthy relationships. It is not a "take no prisoners" approach or about seeking retribution. Healthy relationships require loyalty, patience, understanding, compassion, and forgiveness. They are rooted in love. Leaders demonstrate love for the people with whom they work by helping them reach their full potential in contributing to a cause larger than their own self-interest. And leaders do this by exhibiting patience as their staff learns the new literacies required in this test-driven accountability era.

Finally, leadership engages the human spirit. It requires the spirit of creativity, imagination, and wonder. It requires moral purpose and alignment in pursuing noble goals and virtue. It lives in wisdom's house and nurtures the innate goodness of people and life. It rejoices in the wonder of the universe and life itself and uplifts our souls in the face of events. It challenges us to learn and celebrate life no matter our circumstances. It calls us to be happy and to find our calling without regard to our attachments or the expectations of others. It calls us to live our lives vigorously and courageously.

Soft leadership is required to build relationships that will successfully address the challenges we face. Success, quantitative or qualitative, rests on the interconnected relationships we create between those we lead and ourselves.

The true bottom line for schools or other organizations is found and characterized in several ways.

- *Synergy*—Is the whole greater than the sum of the parts? Leadership develops organizations that exceed the individual potential of the people within it. People are not parts. Collective action should supercede the individual ability of each person. Some organizations perform below their potential because leaders were hardheaded or wrongheaded in nurturing an individual's potential.
- *Talent*—Leadership increases the organizational and individual capacity to create, to respond, to develop, to build, and to succeed. Some leaders do not build the skills, knowledge, or relationships required for success.
- *Creativity*—Do people feel free to find solutions creatively and innovatively? Are they intimidated by failure? Do they rigidly stick to plans and fear improvising? Do they act with integrity regarding values and mission? Are they victims or players?
- *Success*—Do people feel a sense of commitment and obligation? Do they ensure that the organization is not simply effective at mindless and irrelevant things? Do they ensure that the values and moral obligation of the profession are maintained? Are they courageous and safe in presenting dissenting opinion and thinking outside of the box?

Leadership is a huge obligation that ties cognitive ventures with matters of heart and soul. Leadership requires hard data and information for assessing growth and it also requires soft hearts and great spirit for successful, committed relationships, and courageous and intuitive decisions in the face of terrific challenges. A set of processes and a computer that crunches data and presents metrical analysis and mathematical models for behavior in social systems is just not up to the task. It is a necessary condition for success, but alone it is insufficient—in fact, without the softer side of leadership, it is dangerous.

Challenging times require a soft, deft, and human response of the head, heart, and spirit. Anything less will just add to the harshness and dehumanization of our organizations and life itself.

Index

About the Authors

Philip A. Streifer, Ph.D., is associate professor of Educational Leadership at the NEAG School of Education, University of Connecticut, where he directs and teaches the Executive Leadership Program for superintendency preparation and certification. He is also program coordinator for the school's educational administration programs. His research interests include how educational organizations improve in a data-driven rich environment, and he has spoken and published on this topic nationally. He has served as superintendent of schools in Avon, Connecticut, and Barrington, Rhode Island, before joining the University of Connecticut and has held building and district level leadership positions in several Connecticut and Rhode Island school districts. Dr. Streifer holds a Ph.D. and CAGS in Educational Administration from the University of Connecticut, a Master's Degree from Central Connecticut State University in School Administration, and a Bachelor's Degree in Music Education from the Hartt School, The University of Hartford. He is the author of *Using Data to Make Better Educational Decisions* (ScarecrowEducation), and is also president of his own firm, EDsmart, Inc., which provides information technologies to schools nationally.

George A. Goens, Ph.D., has served at all levels of public education and has consulted with organizations on leadership, management, and program evaluation. He is senior partner with Goens/Esparo, LLC, a leadership consulting and executive search firm. In addition, he is a professional associate with the Connecticut Association of Public School Superintendents.

Dr. Goens has led and managed significant organizations. He served as superintendent of two Wisconsin districts for over thirteen years. He also taught social studies, served as principal at the middle school level, and served as director of personnel in a school district of over 500 employees.

He was an associate professor in the doctoral program in educational leadership at the University of Hartford for five years. His research interests include leadership, organizational theory, the superintendency, chaos and complexity theory, and organizational change and reform.

In his consulting practice, he has worked with policy-making boards in evaluating and finding quality leaders and managers. In addition, he has trained leaders in decision making, motivation, leadership, and ethics, and he has analyzed and evaluated programs, and assisted clients with administrative restructuring. Dr. Goens worked with public schools and nonprofit boards and agencies providing educational and social services.

Dr. Goens has written two books and has published fifty-one articles on leadership, management, ethics, change, and motivation.